The Cow Jumped Over The Moon

The Cow Jumped Over The Moon

The Writing and Reading of Poetry

Earle Birney

Holt, Rinehart and Winston of Canada, Limited

Distributed in the United States of America by Winston Press, Minneapolis.

Cover Design: Gail Geltner

ISBN 0-03-923361-8 (Text)
ISBN 0-03-929989-9 (Trade)

Distributed in the United States of America by
Winston Press,
25 Groveland Terrace,
Minneapolis, Minnesota 55403

Published simultaneously in Great Britain by
Holt-Blond, Limited,
120 Golden Lane,
Barbican,
London E.C.1Y OTU, England.

Printed in Canada
1 2 3 4 5   76 75 74 73 72

for bet
& for tony & donna
& all who help others
to see their own cows
jumping the moon

ACKNOWLEDGEMENTS

HARCOURT BRACE JOVANOVICH, INC. For permission to quote from "anyone lived in a pretty how town" from *Poems 1923-1954*, by e. e. cummings.

JONATHAN CAPE LTD. For permission to quote from "The K," from *The Archaelogist of Morning* by Charles Olson. Published by Cape Goliard Press.

NEW DIRECTIONS PUBLISHING CORP. For permission to quote from "The K," *Selected Writings*, Charles Olson. Reprinted by permission of New Directions Publishing Corporation.

THE SWALLOW PRESS INC. Shinkichi Takahashi. "Words," translated by Lucien Stryk reprinted from *Afterimages: Zen Poems of Shinkichi Takahashi* © 1970 by permission of The Swallow Press, Chicago.

McCLELLAND AND STEWART LTD. For permission to reprint "David," "Ellesmereland I," "Ellesmereland II," and "El Greco: Espolio" from *Selected Poems* by Earle Birney reprinted by permission of The Canadian Publishers McClelland and Stewart Limited, Toronto.

DAVID HIGHAM ASSOCIATES, LTD. For permission to quote from "The Force That Through the Green Fuse" from *Selected Poems* by Dylan Thomas.

TALONBOOKS. For permission to quote from "Seeing is Seeing is Believing in Poetry" from *A Few Myths* by Peter Stevens. Reprinted by permission of the author and Talonbooks.

OLWYN HUGHES. For permission to quote from "Daddy" from *Ariel* by Sylvia Plath, copyright © Ted Hughes, 1966.

FABER AND FABER LTD. For permission to quote from "Bagpipe Music" from *The Collected Poems of Louis MacNeice* by Louis MacNeice.

OXFORD UNIVERSITY PRESS, INC. For permission to quote from "Bagpipe Music" from *The Collected Poems of Louis MacNeice*, edited by E. R. Dodds. Copyright © The Estate of Louis MacNeice, 1966. Reprinted by permission of Oxford University Press, Inc.

SOCIETE ANONYME LIBRAIRIE GALLIMARD. For permission to quote from "Le Cimetière Marin" from *Charmes* by Paul Valéry.

KENNETH REXROTH. For permission to quote from a letter to Earle Birney.

AL PURDY. For permission to quote from a letter to Earle Birney.

MRS. J. K. THOMAS. For permission to quote from a letter to Earle Birney by J. K. Thomas.

HAROLD DEW. For permission to quote from a letter to Earle Birney, 5 May, 1960.

CONTENTS

1 WRITING POETRY

Who often reads, will sometimes wish to write.

George Crabbe

*Another damned, thick, square book! Always
scribble, scribble, scribble! Eh! Mr. Gibbon?*

Wm. Henry, Duke of Gloucester

This book is mostly about a poem I wrote called "David." I
begin by recalling the making of it: the happenings, thoughts,
motives, influences that led me first to the idea and then to
the shaping of it. Then I talk about the difficulties I had in
finding readers and listeners. This in turn leads me to a
discussion of the problems others have encountered in reading
the poem, especially those caught in the process of having it
taught to them. This book, in fact, is intended to be even more
about "creative" reading than "creative" writing.

Why "creative"? I've put quotes around this word because
in a sense all writing could be creative, and all reading too. In
today's world, however, much writing merely appeals to old
attitudes and standard emotional responses by using phrases
and ideas long familiar. Examples are the cliché language of
politics and of most (but not all) advertising and journalism.
Good "uncreative" writing may be concerned chiefly with an
impersonal recording of facts or a predominantly logical,
unemotional approach to ideas; for example, the language of
law, science, history and education. What this book is concerned with is writing made out of a *need* to record, and a *hope*
of sharing. This is the language of the imagination, set

down sometimes in a passionate rush, sometimes in slow struggle with the craft of words. For me, there's a basic joy in the act and the purpose of such writing. That, and the possible pleasure it may bring to others, reading or listening and turning on with their own imaginations, are probably its only "uses."

> *There are many ways, but the Way is mysterious.*
> *There are names but not nature in words*
> *and the source of creation is nameless.*
> *But creatures have a mother and she has a name.*
>
> **Lao Tzu**

The wistful purpose of this book then is to persuade anyone literate in the English language who thinks he does not like poetry that he's missing a unique pleasure easily within his reach—and anyone who likes poetry a little, or only some kinds of poems, that he may extend his range and his pleasures.

However, students are warned (*kaff! kaff!*) that I consider the "teaching" of poetry a perversion of the intentions of poets; that I denounce *(harumph!)* any teachers or professors who make this book the *sole* text for any course, or who set examinations on it requiring a "right" answer. Persons employing this text for authoritarian purposes are the enemies of all genuine students. The latter are hereby cautioned that this book is based on nine personal and probably unsound premises about the nature of poetry:

1. a poem is an art object, something begun in personal fancy and developed by a kind of serious play

2. it is therefore unreliable as a source of information about its subject or its author, on any rational level

3. it is a survival of primitive spells and exorcisms, and cannot be entered into by anyone who has excluded wonder and mystery from his life

4. it is the use of words to combine the pleasures of music and dancing, and so cannot be adequately enjoyed without being heard in the inner ear at least, and felt in the body's rhythms

5. virtually all human beings are born with the abilities needed to delight in and to make poetry, but unimaginative concepts of education can muffle and even destroy these abilities

6. the essential "education" for both a poet (and his reader) is exploring indefinitely his medium, understanding words as they are spoken and written, and especially as they have been shaped into the poetry of his generation

7. this education begins naturally with the lullaby and the nursery rhyme, and it can continue in the school only if the teachers offer so-called adult poetry in the same childish spirit of sharing the magic of rhythm and fancy, and of expecting no more from it than pleasure, comfort, and perhaps reconciliation with the darker moments of being alive

8. the best "teachers" of poetry are therefore those who attempt not to teach but to be fellow students and practitioners in the making and enjoying of an imaginative craft

9. "courses" in poetry are of no use without provision of the real things: books of poetry, disks, tapes, and films incorporating it (without censorship on the score of content or language); programs involving readings of poetry by the poets themselves or by imaginative readers; and discussions (not "classes") with poets and other artists in relaxed situations and settings

Further warning: the above statements are all partly false. They are simply the momentary verbalizations of one very fallible human being, me, phrased on a night in August 1971, rephrased on a September morning, and again on a February afternoon in 1972. I may yet revise them again before they see print, or regret that I didn't. It would help students of poetry a great deal if they remembered always that *anything* they read is likely to be only half-true at best. There's no one meaning to any authentic poem, no one interpretation valid for everybody, no value judgment that the passage of history won't render invalid.

In other words, never quite believe anything until you've checked inside yourself, as well as outside, to know if it is true for you. Print has no authority *per se*.

Everyone is alone with the poem.

Andrei Voznesensky

The only thing reasonably accurate in this book you are presently reading is the text of the poem "David," and proof errors may have slipped by even there. Even the best firms make them.

And now it's high time I explained why I'm talking mainly about "David." Many poets have written better poems. Even I have, I think. The answer is threefold:

1. Of all the three hundred-odd poems I've published, this is the one that's been most widely read, critically discussed, anthologized and "taught." At one time or another in the last twenty-five years, it's been required reading for high schools and/or universities in every Canadian province. Consequently, I've received many letters about it from students and from teachers. So I've more information about "teaching problems" and methods and reactions in relation to this poem, and I can discuss it with greater assurance of a prior knowledge of the text among readers of this book. (The text is nevertheless supplied; I'm not taking any chances.)

2. It was a difficult poem to get published, and I've kept a record of those difficulties.

3. I happen to remember a good deal about the way the poem began in my head and this book is first of all about

The Writing of Poems (or at least why I wrote "David")

I suppose writing was a habit I'd already got into, as a natural follow-up to reading. I spent my first seven years on a bush farm in central Alberta, an only child and much alone. My parents taught me to listen quite early to selections from the Bible and to read from the newspapers—especially *The Family Herald and Weekly Star*—that came in a weekly bundle up at the flag station's post office. By the time we had sold up and moved within access of a school, I'd discovered Burns' *Poetical Works* hidden in my mother's bureau, got launched through *Darkest Africa with Stanley & Livingstone*, started a diary and secretly decided to be a writer. Also a missionary. And a doctor, of course.

However, after five years of schooling, I realized that all writers were products of other countries, or at least of the unknown Canadian East. In any case my teachers had, without trying, convinced me that literature was a bore. I decided to go for Stanley and journalism, and became founding editor, at twelve, of a realistic underground school paper. Handwritten and illustrated, it existed in three copies—I had two assistant editors—and was rented, not sold. Our lady teacher intercepted a copy and passed it to the principal who agreed with her judgment that it was pornographic. This certainly described our intention, and in that respect we were successful communicators, but in 1916 our sole reward was the cat-of-nine-tails.

From then until I left high school, I wrote only what the teacher assigned, essays on the Plantagenet Kings or Longfellow's *Hiawatha*, and I dutifully memorized such examination pieces as "The Arab's Farewell to his Faithful Steed" and other versified tear jerkers. Even in my knockabout years as a labourer, between high school and college, I wrote nothing but a few lugubrious lyrics in the style of Gray's "Elegy in a Country Churchyard."

I registered in a university to become a chemical engineer or maybe a geologist. After my second year I switched to the Honours program in English Literature. This, I think now, was a mistake, even or especially for a poet. No doubt the courses forced me to read through the major poems of English literature, but I was acquiring just such a reading background on my own and would have gone on doing so without the artificial stimulus of essays and examinations—and at the same time would have fitted myself for an economically sound career in chemical warfare.

A losing trade, I assure you, sir: literature is a drug.

George Borrow

Certainly I would have escaped being brainwashed by my professors of English into thinking it an indiscretion on my part to divert spare time energies into writing poetry or fiction — unless, of course, what I was producing would be immediately acclaimed by the world as works of genius. Since my tutors were united in assuring me to the contrary, I burned most of my verses; a few I published in student journals under pseudonyms. Still, the scribbling habit persisted.

My writing in the next fourteen years consisted of:

(a) longer and longer essays and exams on other writers safely dead, culminating in a nine hundred-page doctoral thesis, quite unpublishable

(b) probably about one hundred thousand words of hurried and largely unheeded criticism in the margins of students' essays

(c) about a hundredweight of seminar notes and outlines for half a dozen courses I was myself teaching

(d) another hundred pounds or so of course outlines, reviews, and essays pedantic or political.

Poems? In all that time scarcely a dozen, and nearly all trivia. But in 1940 life took a new turn for me. Fascist armies were conquering Europe and massacring Poles, Jews, socialists. I had a wife and son now, both Jews, with Polish relatives, and we were all socialists. I began training in the Canadian Army while still a teacher in the University of Toronto; since I could see years ahead in which my energies would be totally absorbed by the war or ended by it, I commenced at the same time to set down a few short poems in a spirit of bitter hail-and-farewell to the lost days of peace. Some of them were liked by one or two editors in Toronto who shared my feelings without being caught up in patriotic hysteria. The poems were published, and I was encouraged to tackle something a little bigger.

There was still a work I had not got at, an area of my experience I longed to contain in words while I still had a chance. I didn't yet know what it was, even whether it was to be in verse or prose, but it had to be something that moved beyond the immediate dualities of war and peace into a world more universal, and yet also more personal. I was now thirty-six years old. I began to see that it was the passing of my youth I was mourning, which peace would not bring back, not to me nor to any of my generation. I felt a deep need, a compulsion, to express this inevitable change from carefree happiness, this loss that none escapes unless he die young.

> *Happy men do not make literature.*
>
> *Franz Kafka*

In my case I had lost both my youngness and that western wilderness which had made my early joys so rare and intense. Or so I say now, long after. In 1940 I was not so prosily aware of what I was feeling; the poem was still a vague fluid washing around in my mind.

Then one day that autumn it began to crystallize. I'd put in a full day's teaching, rushed home to supper and was hurrying back along Bloor Street (dressed now in the khaki of an infantry private), for an evening of hated rifle drill. As I walked, I began enjoying the grand snows and glaciers of a high mountain at the flat street's end, caught in the rose of sunset. Suddenly I realized it was only a freak of the clouds—and of my mind. No one else on the street was doing a double take.

I was overwhelmed with insight into my obsession, into what I had to write about before the army bore me out of Canada. Mountains. I had to unburden myself about mountains—their beauty and their hostility; about my peaks and all the sweating exhilarations and adventures and shivers of climbing them; about the misadventures, small as mine had been.

It was the duality of those Rockies—like the war, both challenging and treacherous—or better, it was the duality of Man I was after. It's not stone that lures and betrays, but man the animal, carrying within him both zest and grief, youth and age, love and hate, life and death. It wasn't, please note, that I wanted to make moral comments like "gather ye rosebuds while ye may" or "beware the awful avalanche" or anything else designed to change a reader's life-style. I simply wanted to represent certain realities of life which the climbing of mountains could symbolize. And above all, I wanted to make the mountains as real in words as they had continued to be in wordless memory in my mind.

But there were too many mountains in my memory: I'd begun my scrambles on the slopes above Banff at the age of seven, and for the next fifteen years I'd scarcely ever been out of sight of mountains. I'd fished in the canyons of the Kootenays, pack-horsed into lakes in the remoter parts of Banff National Park and guided tourists up its ranges, hunted fossils on cliffs for a museum, strung meteorological cable up Sulphur Mountain, worked as a swamper, rock-driller and ditch-digger around the Vermilion Lakes and as axeman and rodman to surveyors on the Continental Divide. In college days I'd climbed with the B.C. Mountaineering Club and other parties over glaciers and ice-fields on the Pacific, bobsleighed down the mountains of Utah, and rock-climbed in Wales and in the Sierras. How to condense, select, reshape these memories and perceptions between daylong teaching and nightly drilling? How to connect the childish thrills of coming upon a rare alpine flower or glimpsing a new peak, with the sobering "adult" encounters with storms on summits, with grizzlies, with flash floods and rockfalls?

But now I've moved from talking about "why" to the story of

How I Wrote "David"

For by that time the theme and tone had already written themselves. But there was still an immediate decision to be made about shape before I could stop swimming in chaos.

Obviously I had to find some form that was concentrated and symbolic, in the sense that I could use a single action or scene to catch both the small realities and the larger visions I associated with mountains. Perhaps a short story? Certainly I felt I needed human presences, fragments of myselves-when-young, so that I could preserve something individual. But what?

The ordinary preoccupations of my daytime life couldn't be set aside except for an hour or two before sleep, and yet there was a constant welling-up of ideas and now images, demanding attention to memories, to the past. Sensations and actions long "forgotten" began to pop into consciousness again.

It's important, I think, to stress this muddled, slow, irrational nature of the creative process, at least as I experience it in the critical early stages. Limitations of time and space tempt the writers of books such as this to make things sound more reasonable and orderly than they ever are. In the shaping of any of my poems which have succeeded at all, I never really knew what I was doing until it was done, and even then I wasn't sure, and I'm not now. To reach the imaginations of others through mere squiggles on paper, the writer must allow for or submit to *his* imagination taking him over, to entering on a trip of inner discovery and free fantasy in which immediate time is eerily annihilated in a rapture of concentration.

Children know about this and, given freedom, they live poetry and even write it, compose in ways genuinely moving and fresh, each child expressing deep and unique feelings within a small common environment. But their brief memory span and the limitations of their word-knowledge make the poetry even of the infant prodigy unmemorable, however natural and flowing. Though the so-called adult poet may envy the simplicity and ease with which most children, given a little encouragement, can create with words, it's the former's richer memory and vocabulary, and the complexity of the unceasing struggle within him between his developed reason and his childlike fantasizing, which have produced the great passages in *Hamlet*, the odes of Keats, the lyrics of Dylan Thomas.

Mature art, I think, emerges when there's a certain balance of tensions, when there's neither neurotic prostration nor cold rationality, but an aura of energy and a drive to grasp personal "truths" still emerging into perception. To grasp and to shape them. The difference from the child's approach is perhaps one of *form*, a containment instinctively felt but in the end conscious.

*They are ill discouerers that think there is
no land, when they can see nothing but sea.*

Francis Bacon

In these respects I suspect the mature artist is no different from the creative scientist, the mathematician, the explorer, the philosopher. All are energized by an obsession to make real and clear and formally memorable what began as only a cloudy guess. The creative experience is psychedelic in its beginnings but it becomes a "good trip" only if it moves eventually into the discovery of final form, into a sense of completing, of saying something as well as one can. There is a movement from mind-stretching to mind-controlling, from a mere swimming about in chaos to a search for land.

The Finding of Form

The writing of a poem *is* the search for its precise form, a series of decisions about "shape."

First, with "David," was it to be drama or non-drama? An easy answer: my subject was visually too grandiose, and humanly too restricted, to be natural on a stage. Non-dramatic, then.

Second, poetry or prose? More difficult to decide. The difference is not simply a visual matter of choosing between a solid right margin with paragraph breaks versus an irregular right margin and line breaks—even if many readers seem willing to believe anything broken up is verse and anything solid "only" prose. No, if I have my writing set in verse lines, I'm signalling to my readers that I'm about to use any of a number of techniques he doesn't normally expect to find in English prose and that indeed many prose writers consciously avoid.

Before I go farther, I want to set down what I consider to be these special techniques to be expected in most poetry:

1. *Sound effects* intended, in part, to make the poem carry pleasures not only to the inner ear, but to others hearing it

spoken or even chanted or sung. Traditional among such effects are:

(a) *strong rhythms* or pulsations, repeated regularly or irregularly and indicated by line breaks, with sometimes the aid of spaces within lines and of punctuation

It's no go the merrygoround, it's no go the rickshaw,

(b) *musical cadences* by means of rhymes, vowel or consonant chimings (assonance, consonance, alliteration) or equivalent discords, through a false-rhyme and dissonance

All we want is a limousine and a ticket for the peepshow.

Louis MacNeice: *Bagpipe Music*

2. *Repetitions* of key words, often with meaning shifts, and of dominant images and ideas, for purposes not only of emphasis (as in rhetorical prose) but of producing effects in the nature of "spells" and "exorcisms"; a form of transference of what is haunting the poet into writing, to a haunting of those who read

The boot in the face, the brute
Brute heart of a brute like you.

Sylvia Plath: *Daddy*

3. *Concentrated expression:* the fewest possible words/ sounds to say the most intended. No syllable without a function

Parting is all we know of heaven,
And all we need of hell.

Emily Dickinson: *#1732*

4. *Total verbal freedom* to use whatever kind of grammar and whatever level of word the poet feels will best convey his own true voice and the exact shades of meaning he intends. Syntax, the conventions of word order, all the solemn rules of college texts on "good English" are followed or ignored in the interest

of effectiveness. "The best words in the best order." A drawing upon the total vocabulary of the English language, what our Anglo-Saxon ancestors called the "word-hoard." Words are the poet's medium, to be expended as the painter uses paint. By words alone the poet must create his colour, music, emotion, thought, his personal universe. In the interests of precision he may use technical terms, in the interests of atmosphere, archaic or exotic ones; he may need four-letter words or fourteeners, puns and other ambiguities, understatements to make over-feelings, words particularly charged by their original meanings, sudden leaps in thought, paradoxes, contradictions and fantastic challenges to the reader's imagination

> I caught this morning morning's minion, kingdom of
> daylight's dauphin, dapple-dawn-drawn Falcon, . . .
>
> G. M. Hopkins: *The Windhover*

> anyone lived in a pretty how town . . . ,
> he sang his didn't he danced his did.
>
> e. e. cummings: *anyone lived . . .*

5.   Despite all these sophistications, the surface clarity of a mountain stream (permitting glimpses of swirling depths, however, and hints of strange shadows and movements below). *The art of appearing simple and offering complexity,* leading the reader down from the word to the image to the symbol, and from the poet and his disguises, his "characters," to the reader's most secret self

> The night has a love for throwing its shadows around a man
> a bridge, a horse, the gun, a grave.
>
> Charles Olson: *The K*

6.   An assumption that readers and listeners will be willing and able to project beyond the poet's immediate thought, to draw on all their own resources of intelligence, sensitivity and human intuition, to explore their own subconscious, to match or excel the poet's — in short, to write their own poems while

reading and listening to his. Dylan Thomas talked about "a main column of meaning" in his poems. It's the river image again. It's there in all but the dadaistic anti-poems; it carries the reader along with the poem, but is full of rapids and back currents. Every reader has to find his own way down to the sea. The poet writes out of *a faith in the existence of at least one reader,* someone who can share his vision and, yes, his love of humanity. Though we now seem to be creatures destined to destroy ourselves within a generation, we humans have within us still the power to rescue ourselves and all life. Poets are generally among the sharpest critics of existing civilization and societies but when a poet comes to believe that man is totally evil and without hope, he won't seek any longer for a reader. However, he'll continue to write.

> And I am dumb to tell the lover's tomb
> How at my sheet goes the same crooked worm.

> Dylan Thomas: *The force that through*
> *the green fuse . . .*

7.   This is because, for all his care to involve his audience, *a poet is in the first place writing for himself.* The act is a kind of confrontation and self-exploration done partly in an agony of search, partly in euphoric excitement, out of the fiercest honesty.

> ### Profound sincerity is the only basis of talent, as of character.
> #### Ralph Waldo Emerson

The poem, to be sure, is generally written down, and often recited; so there's ultimately an intent to communicate. But what is offered is not the pain but the pleasure of the art of words. The offering is free. Poets don't write for money, since almost any other occupation pays better. Nor do poets expect any but the most transitory "fame," especially in this twentieth century, which may well be man's last on his radioactive earth-ship. Poems are written compulsively, as Robinson Crusoe wrote a diary without being sure anyone would ever read it. If I were marooned on an island I'd scratch poems on the sands for want of pencil and paper, and watch the tide erase them. I might try to memorize them first, just in case, but my real satisfaction would come from the act of creation itself.

I've set down at some length these differences between poetry and prose, so far as I understand their attitudes and techniques, because it seems to me a quite reasonable question to ask why a poet makes any particular idea into a poem. A Grade 11 student in a Toronto collegiate one year put it bluntly indeed to his teacher in respect to my "David": "Wouldn't that story have been better written in prose?" And I had a feeling once, talking about the poem with Morley Callaghan, that he was inclined to the same query. However, though "David" is cast in almost traditional short-story form, the impulses behind it were, as I've already indicated, only secondarily narrative. I was happy to hear from that Grade 11 teacher that she had referred the question to her class for a debate at the next meeting, and they'd decided to go along with "David" the way it was. If most readers felt it would be better as prose I would know the poem had failed, failed both them and me. The questioning student, it developed, just liked anything in prose better, and wanted to see "David" made really good.

There's no reason, of course, why the poem could not have been given a prose form, or a musical or dramatic or cinematic one. It was in fact converted to an oratorio by the Canadian composer, Lorne Betts, and there's presently an option on it for a film short. Many unhappy students have been compelled to make prose paraphrases of it. It may well be that these metamorphoses are improvements on the original but I'd be too prejudiced a witness to know. I'm not suggesting that my poem is sacrosanct, only that I thought of my theme as something highly emotional, yet contained within realistic narrative, something that would begin with a lyrical celebration of the joys of mountain climbing in youth, and turn, on a dramatic climax, into a sinister re-viewing of those scenes in an atmosphere of tragedy. It had to be something which evoked "real" experience and then reshaped, distorted, even contradicted

14

that ordinary reality in the interests of an over-all vision of the personal truths propelling me into writing.

> *Still, it is not a window, it isn't just glass;*
> *see with, not through the eye. See the way*
> *things look, not the way we know things are.*
>
> Peter Stevens

I couldn't, if I'd wanted, have made it a painting or a dance. It plainly wasn't a documentary, or a showing of colour slides. It must be a piece of writing moving from precise realities into the universals of space. It had to be a poem and, if you like, a narrative poem.

But before I could write a line of it I had to work out at least the gist of my

Poetic Narrative

Where should it be set? By 1940 I'd been up a lot of mountains and my theme was about man, anywhere. If what I sought was a wide audience, I should place the poem in the United States, particularly since I'd discovered by now that American editors were highly unreceptive to material betraying a Canadian origin — unless the subjects were mounties, huskies and northern badmen. But popularity was not my concern or I wouldn't have set out to write a poem of any kind, and certainly not a narrative one.

In the thirties and forties fashionable critics had decreed that narrative poetry was a naive form, its days gone forever with epic heroes and all that. Long poems now had to be learned and philosophical, with footnotes. T. S. Eliot's "The Waste Land" was still in, but the *Canterbury Tales*, Browning, Frost, and E. J. Pratt were out. Poets, however, are much less apt to be fashion-followers than their critics. In 1940 I was in quite conscious rebellion against those pedantic, over-intellectual verse writers who undervalued clarity, loved elegant mystifications and reduced poetry to a cold wordplay with negative emotions. I wanted to talk about the positive joys and loves of life, as well as about the loss of them. Moreover, I'd always made my deepest poetic devotion to Chaucer and Blake, Shakespeare and Wordsworth and Yeats, rather than to Pope or Auden. For me, Coleridge's "Rime of the Ancient Mariner," Keats' "Eve of St. Agnes," *Sir Gawain and the Green Knight* and the *Beowulf* are all great poems, and no less great because they are narratives.

So it was to be a story and one set in Canada, in the high Rockies; not because I wanted to be a nationalist poet but because the Canadian mountains were the ones I knew best, and the ones that, up to that time, no poet had written about.

To simplify matters, I decided to have my characters spend a summer in and around a single mountain valley, which would remain nameless. Then I moved the mountains I wanted from anywhere — several from the B.C. Coast, a couple from Waterton Lakes, one from Utah's Wasatches — and arranged them with some peaks around the Bow Valley between Canmore and Lake Louise. I wasn't writing a travelogue, or autobiography; I imported details and incidents from other climbs, so long as they *could* have happened in the Bow Valley. I preserved geographical names only when the names had the sound and sense I wanted; otherwise I gave real mountains better names than they had; but the climactic mountain I invented, rock, name and chimney.

Time? No great problem — the twenties would do, when I was young and climbing hardest. The nature of the setting and its remoteness in a protected wilderness gave it a certain timelessness, which may have prevented the poem's visualities looking too much out of date even in the polluted seventies.

What about *plot*, the action? Well, it had to concretize that theme of the duality of mountains which I'd already chosen, and also the duality of experience to be encountered by men who roam in them. A double doubleness. . . .

> *Veil after veil will lift—but there must be*
> *Veil upon veil behind.*
> **Edwin Arnold**

I now began to see the first half of the poem as a varied series of climbs extending through the centre of a summer, the climber's high season. The action would be relatively uneventful, the details selected to build a sense of youthful zest. I'd first try to make everyone, whether they'd ever seen a mountain or not, feel how wonderful it is to be alive and strong and adventuring among mountains. But there would need to be some details loaded with ironies, with symbols foreshadowing a reversal to grief and disaster, blending the youthful romanticism with an increasingly realistic understanding of life. And I would try to shape these emblems to be fully understood only when the poem was ended.

The second half would be a single event taking place on one mountain in the course of about twenty-four hours, the old Greek unities of time, place and action. But there would still be a duality; first a movement of the climbers through timber and up the eerie beauties of summer snowfields, glacial crevasses, seracs and snowbridges, to the challenges of the rocky spires and the climactic triumph of standing on what had been an unclimbed peak. Then would come what the Greeks called a *peripetia*, a sudden reversal of fortune — literally, a fall.

But someone must survive, I now could see, to describe the descent. By using a narrator who remained to carry on the action, I could picture the same scenes, first in the exhilaration and élan of the ascent, and then in the horror of the return; every detail the same, so far as nature was concerned, but looking entirely different now, from the viewpoint of the shocked, lonely, desperate survivor. This one will never move again in mountains with unthinking boyish acceptance of the pleasures they offer. From now on, memories of pain and wasteful death will remain interwoven with his keenest pleasures.

Again, let the student beware. The poem did not evolve in as orderly a fashion as all that. I swam blindly a long time in the chaos into which I'd dived, before I could make out land. This is as close as my memory can come now to the process. At least I'm sure the poem did grow in a strange way from theme to plot to character — a reverse order from that into which I've been led when writing any of my prose stories.

Characters last, then, and only one to survive. How many others? I could see no reason for more than two people in the story. I was not portraying professional mountaineers, who usually travel in threes or more on ropes for greater safety and other technical reasons. Here two was right; they should be close friends since the emotional impact on the survivor would be strengthened. (And now I was beginning to think consciously of an accident that had happened to someone I knew, and whose story had been slowly making its way up from my subconscious memory; of this, more in a moment.) One is killed, or permanently disabled. The other, unhurt, goes all the way back to camp alone.

Who is he, the survivor? Someone in his teens at the time, telling the story later but when still young, the memory of it fresh and real, his emotions still loyal to his past. He must be this way for he's the voice of the poem, and the poem is not about old age but about youth suddenly shocked into adultness. Should he be the older of the two, the more experienced climber surviving because of superior skill or prudence? No, the tragedy would be all the deeper if the leader were the victim. My next thought was that irony and extra intensity would be gained if Bob (as I began to call my younger one, an "anybody" name) were both the hero-worshipping follower and, somehow, by his lack of skill, a cause of his leader's death.

Now real-life incidents, about which I had heard, began to crowd in on me. One was the death in the twenties of a fellow undergraduate in the mountains on the edge of Vancouver. I had never climbed with him, and only read a fragmentary news account of the accident later. It seems he had slipped backwards on a rocky slope, had fallen perhaps only fifteen feet and broken his spine. His single companion, unable to move him, had gone down the mountain for help. Although he guided rescuers back within eight hours and it was summertime, the boy was found dead of his injuries, complicated by exposure. I appropriated his name, David, for my title and leading figure. What little I knew of the original David's character went into that of his namesake's: courage, steadiness, honesty, capacity for self-sacrifice, love of the game for the game's sake.

WARNING: I didn't proceed as analytically as this; rather, I continued developing my story and shaping my character to be believeable in terms of the events. My David in consequence became daring, proud, intense, romantic — a man who knew instantly, once he had to choose, that he preferred immediate death to a slow one waiting for rescuers who could save him only for a lifetime in a wheelchair, if they could arrive in time even for that.

I had then to mould my Bob into such a worshipful follower of this David that he would, though not without agonies of hesitation beforehand and remorse after, actually give his helpless friend the *coup de grâce* he was begging for. I made this solution easier to accept, I think, by emphasizing the remoteness of the scene from help, and the lethal hostility of high mountain weather. But I could see that the climax would not be fully convincing unless I thought myself into Bob's mind, shared his most harrowing of decisions, became him.

The use of first person narration, upon which I'd already decided, helped me to identify more naturally with this imagined character. I knew, for instance, that Bob would feel even more guilty about his carelessness on the peak, which had precipitated the tragedy, than about his act of euthanasia.

The idea of David falling immediately after he'd reached the peak and untied the rope came to me from a newspaper account of an accident on Mount Eon, a rocky spire near the Bugaboos of British Columbia, from which an American mountaineer fell to his death. His companion was his wife, whom he was preparing to belay up the summit from the last ledge. She remained on it, unable to descend alone, and was found by a rescue party barely in time to prevent her death from exposure.

It was from others' misfortunes that I had to draw the main action of my story since I'm happy to say that in all the climbs I took part in through my life, neither I nor my companions ever suffered so much as a broken bone. Autobiography, despite what the literal-minded assume and have encouraged others to believe, played no role in the climactic episode. However, by an ironic twist, a "real-life" story with some parallels to "David" happened to my own son when he and his closest friend, another teen-ager, were climbing a small rock-face in mountains near Vancouver, without ropes, at dusk. His friend slipped and fell about thirty feet, fracturing his skull and sliding into a bog. My son had to drag his comrade out of the mire, then leave him unconscious and go many miles in darkness through tangled woods before he found help. But all this happened twenty-five years after I wrote my poem; life, in Oscar Wilde's phrase, had imitated art. In this case, however, my son's friend was lifted at dawn by helicopter and was recovering in a city hospital within another hour.

Everything I've said so far has been about the composing of "David" inside my head, as I walked to and from the nearby University of Toronto in the daytime and to the drillfields after supper. Actually, "churning" would be more accurate than "composing," for I was still revolving over and over a cloudy liquid of facts and ideas, memories and fancies, images and perceptions. But on paper I had only gobs of prosy notes.

Indeed the actual writing could scarcely begin until I knew what was to be the poem's form as it would appear on the page and be heard in the ear, its

Verbal Patterns and Rhythms

The decisions about these had to come naturally from the ones already made about overall form, subject, setting, action, characters.

Obviously I needed a flexible metre to span the two widely separated moods of the poem which moved from carefree high spirits to numb disaster. A rhythm of ups and downs, then, but not bumping or dragging, always moving ahead.

It was at this point I began consciously to profit from the examples of some narrative poets whose techniques I'd admired. There was Stephen Vincent Benét and his *John Brown's Body*. But the great metrical variety maintained in that poem, through constantly changing stanzaic patterns, could happen only within the length of a book. Mine was to have the nature of a short short story, needing to keep to whatever was its basic rhythm in order not to blur the "single effect." The verse tragedies of Robinson Jeffers, on the other hand, so grandly mournful, were too much in monotone for my taste. The

Conquistador of Archibald MacLeish, though also a much longer poem, was nearer to what I wanted. His mingling of anapests and iambs and amphibrachs produced effects of strength and zest as well as cadences of helplessness and sorrow: that combination could stagger, even crawl, or it could move, as Coleridge said, "with a leap and a bound." MacLeish had controlled his rhythm with assonance or vowel-rhyme, a device with which I had become familiar when I studied Old French in the graduate school of the University of California and read the eleventh Century *Chanson de Roland* in the original. I now reread it, and it helped me to weave my own sound-form, a dividend from my Berkeley days.

As soon as I began shaping lines, I had to make a decision about stanzas. The reader's eye becomes oppressed by pages of solid type (how many pages I didn't know). And yet I wanted a sense of continuous flow. I decided then to have stanza eye-breaks, but to keep both rhythm and sense flowing, with only the most natural breath-breaks, forward from line to line and line-group to line-group — what the French call *enjambement*.

This process did produce an adventurous pace, but it was a little too fast. It would not create in the voice of Bob that sense of recall, that feeling of the adult looking back, sobered by a tragedy still obsessive in his memory, which my structure required. The poem must be his counterspell against the madness of remembering. I thought of Chaucer, remembering perhaps the passions and agonies of his own youth in *Troilus and Criseyde*, and of Coleridge's "Rime of the Ancient Mariner," where echoing rhyme produces these effects. But I was afraid that much rhyme would slow the story, even distract from it. And yet no rhyme at all, such as in blank verse, might be too wooden. I decided to make an assonantal pattern of *abba* for my stanzas and hold to it throughout. I think if "David" does create moods of nostalgia and fatality, celebrating youthful heroism and yet elegizing its loss, it's partly because of the sonorous cadences these technical devices produce. So the poem is in debt to earlier poets who showed us all how such things can be done.

David

I

David and I that summer cut trails on the survey,
All week in the valley for wages, in air that was steeped
In the wail of mosquitoes, but over the sunalive week-ends
We climbed, to get from the ruck of the camp, the surly

Poker, the wrangling, the snoring under the fetid
Tents, and because we had joy in our lengthening coltish
Muscles, and mountains for David were made to see over,
Stairs from the valleys and steps to the sun's retreats.

II

Our first was Mount Gleam. We hiked in the long afternoon
To a curling lake and lost the lure of the faceted
Cone in the swell of its sprawling shoulders. Past
The inlet we grilled our bacon, the strips festooned

On a poplar prong, in the hurrying slant of the sunset.
Then the two of us rolled in the blanket while round us the cold
Pines thrust at the stars. The dawn was a floating
Of mists till we reached to the slopes above timber, and won

To snow like fire in the sunlight. The peak was upthrust
Like a fist in a frozen ocean of rock that swirled
Into valleys the moon could be rolled in. Remotely unfurling
Eastward the alien prairie glittered. Down through the dusty

Skree on the west we descended, and David showed me
How to use the give of shale for giant incredible
Strides. I remember, before the larches' edge,
That I jumped a long green surf of juniper flowing

Away from the wind, and landed in gentian and saxifrage
Spilled on the moss. Then the darkening firs
And the sudden whirring of water that knifed down a fern-hidden
Cliff and splashed unseen into mist in the shadows.

III

One Sunday on Rampart's arête a rainsquall caught us,
And passed, and we clung by our blueing fingers and bootnails
An endless hour in the sun, not daring to move
Till the ice had steamed from the slate. And David taught me

How time on a knife-edge can pass with the guessing of fragments
Remembered from poets, and naming of strata beside one,
And matching of stories from schooldays. . . . We crawled astride
The peak to feast on the marching ranges flagged

By the fading shreds of the shattered stormcloud. Lingering
There it was David who spied to the south, remote,
And unmapped, a sunlit spire on Sawback, an overhang
Crooked like a talon. David named it the Finger.

That day we chanced on the skull and the splayed white ribs
Of a mountain goat underneath a cliff-face, caught
On a rock. Around were the silken feathers of hawks.
And that was the first I knew that a goat could slip.

IV

And then Inglismaldie. Now I remember only
The long ascent of the lonely valley, the live
Pine spirally scarred by lightning, the slicing pipe
Of invisible pika, and great prints, by the lowest

Snow, of a grizzly. There it was too that David
Taught me to read the scroll of coral in limestone
And the beetle-seal in the shale of ghostly trilobites,
Letters delivered to man from the Cambrian waves.

V

On Sundance we tried from the col and the going was hard.
The air howled from our feet to the smudged rocks
And the papery lake below. At an outthrust we balked
Till David clung with his left to a dint in the scarp,
Lobbed the iceaxe over the rocky lip,

Slipped from his holds and hung by the quivering pick,
Twisted his long legs up into space and kicked
To the crest. Then grinning, he reached with his freckled wrist

And drew me up after. We set a new time for that climb.
That day returning we found a robin gyrating
In grass, wing-broken. I caught it to tame but David
Took and killed it, and said, "Could you teach it to fly?"

VI

In August, the second attempt, we ascended The Fortress,
By the forks of the Spray we caught five trout and fried them
Over a balsam fire. The woods were alive
With the vaulting of mule-deer and drenched with clouds all the morning,

Till we burst at noon to the flashing and floating round
Of the peaks. Coming down we picked in our hats the bright
And sunhot raspberries, eating them under a mighty
Spruce, while a marten moving like quicksilver scouted us.

VII

But always we talked of the Finger on Sawback, unknown
And hooked, till the first afternoon in September we slogged
Through the musky woods, past a swamp that quivered with frog-song,
And camped by a bottle-green lake. But under the cold

Breath of the glacier sleep would not come, the moon-light
Etching the Finger. We rose and trod past the feathery
Larch, while the stars went out, and the quiet heather
Flushed, and the skyline pulsed with the surging bloom

Of incredible dawn in the Rockies. David spotted
Bighorns across the moraine and sent them leaping
With yodels the ramparts redoubled and rolled to the peaks,
And the peaks to the sun. The ice in the morning thaw

Was a gurgling world of crystal and cold blue chasms,
And seracs that shone like frozen saltgreen waves.
At the base of the Finger we tried once and failed. Then David
Edged to the west and discovered the chimney; the last

Hundred feet we fought the rock and shouldered and kneed
Our way for an hour and made it. Unroping we formed
A cairn on the rotting tip. Then I turned to look north
At the glistening wedge of giant Assiniboine, heedless

Of handhold. And one foot gave. I swayed and shouted.
David turned sharp and reached out his arm and steadied me,
Turning again with a grin and his lips ready
To jest. But the strain crumbled his foothold. Without

A gasp he was gone. I froze to the sound of grating
Edge-nails and fingers, the slither of stones, the lone
Second of silence, the nightmare thud. Then only
The wind and the muted beat of unknowing cascades.

VIII

Somehow I worked down the fifty impossible feet
To the ledge, calling and getting no answer but echoes
Released in the cirque, and trying not to reflect
What an answer would mean. He lay still, with his lean

Young face upturned and strangely unmarred, but his legs
Splayed beneath him, beside the final drop,
Six hundred feet sheer to the ice. My throat stopped
When I reached him, for he was alive. He opened his grey

Straight eyes and brokenly murmured, "Over . . . over."
And I, feeling beneath him a cruel fang
Of the ledge thrust in his back, but not understanding,
Mumbled stupidly, "Best not to move," and spoke

Of his pain. But he said, "I can't move. . . . If only I felt
Some pain." Then my shame stung the tears to my eyes
As I crouched, and I cursed myself, but he cried,
Louder, "No, Bobbie! Don't ever blame yourself.

I didn't test my foothold." He shut the lids
Of his eyes to the stare of the sky, while I moistened his lips
From our water flask and tearing my shirt into strips
I swabbed the shredded hands. But the blood slid

From his side and stained the stone and the thirsting lichens,
And yet I dared not lift him up from the gore
Of the rock. Then he whispered, "Bob, I want to go over!"
This time I knew what he meant and I grasped for a lie

And said, "I'll be back here by midnight with ropes
And men from the camp and we'll cradle you out." But I knew
That the day and the night must pass and the cold dews
Of another morning before such men unknowing

The ways of mountains could win to the chimney's top.
And then, how long? And he knew . . . and the hell of hours
After that, if he lived till we came, roping him out.
But I curled beside him and whispered, "The bleeding will stop.

You can last." He said only, "Perhaps. . . . For what? A wheelchair,
Bob?" His eyes brightening with fever upbraided me.
I could not look at him more and said, "Then I'll stay
With you." But he did not speak, for the clouding fever.

I lay dazed and stared at the long valley,
The glistening hair of a creek on the rug stretched
By the firs, while the sun leaned round and flooded the ledge,
The moss, and David still as a broken doll.

I hunched to my knees to leave, but he called and his voice
Now was sharpened with fear. "For Christ's sake push me over!
If I could move . . . or die. . . ." The sweat ran from his forehead,
But only his eyes moved. A hawk was buoying

Blackly its wings over the wrinkled ice.
The purr of a waterfall rose and sank with the wind.
Above us climbed the last joint of the Finger
Beckoning bleakly the wide indifferent sky.

Even then in the sun it grew cold lying there. . . . And I knew
He had tested his holds. It was I who had not. . . . I looked
At the blood on the ledge, and the far valley. I looked
At last in his eyes. He breathed, "I'd do it for you, Bob."

IX

I will not remember how nor why I could twist
Up the wind-devilled peak, and down through the chimney's empty
Horror, and over the traverse alone. I remember
Only the pounding fear I would stumble on It

When I came to the grave-cold maw of the bergschrund . . . reeling
Over the sun-cankered snowbridge, shying the caves
In the névé . . . the fear, and the need to make sure It was there
On the ice, the running and falling and running, leaping

Of gaping greenthroated crevasses, alone and pursued
By the Finger's lengthening shadow. At last through the fanged
And blinding seracs I slid to the milky wrangling
Falls at the glacier's snout, through the rocks piled huge

On the humped moraine, and into the spectral larches,
Alone. By the glooming lake I sank and chilled
My mouth but I could not rest and stumbled still
To the valley, losing my way in the ragged marsh.

I was glad of the mire that covered the stains, on my ripped
Boots, of his blood, but panic was on me, the reek
Of the bog, the purple glimmer of toadstools obscene
In the twilight. I staggered clear to a firewaste, tripped

And fell with a shriek on my shoulder. It somehow eased
My heart to know I was hurt, but I did not faint
And I could not stop while over me hung the range
Of the Sawback. In blackness I searched for the trail by the creek

And found it. . . . My feet squelched a slug and horror
Rose again in my nostrils. I hurled myself
Down the path. In the woods behind some animal yelped.
Then I saw the glimmer of tents and babbled my story.

I said that he fell straight to the ice where they found him.
And none but the sun and incurious clouds have lingered
Around the marks of that day on the ledge of the Finger,
That day, the last of my youth, on the last of our mountains.

Toronto 1940

Drafting and Revising

My sonic form now fairly clear to me, I was able to make a second start. How many beginnings there were before I could drive through to a finished first draft I can't recall, and no one will know, since I destroyed the old ones as I wrote. Many small decisions had still to be made in these rewritings, some unthinking and not always right.

A student once wrote me about "David": "This is one of the few poems in which you capitalize the first letter of a line. Does this serve a purpose or is it just a sign that this was one of your earlier poems?"[1] I had to reply that he was right the second time, for it was long after "David" when I began to look critically at typographical conventions whose effects on the poem-as-seen are often not what the poet intends. But I enjoyed his question; it wasn't a trivial one really, and it showed me that he'd been reading the poem creatively.

---

[1] Letters quoted in this book are on file in the Birney Collection, Rare Books and Manuscripts Section, University of Toronto Library.

To another student's question, as to whether I wrote the poem slowly or "did it fast and then revised it," I could say "both," and ask him in turn "How fast is fast?" It took me two months to finish, but then I could allow myself only an hour or two at the most, and that at the end of a day of giving lectures and preparing new ones, attending committees, drilling, and reading that never-ending flow of student essays the university required me to assign and the students to produce. The first full draft never exceeded the pace of two stanzas a night and a few more on weekends, and as it turned out there were forty-six stanzas.

There were problems still holding me up, besides time and tiredness. Some of them, I remember, had to do with the realism of the setting and action. As I've explained earlier (see p. 16), I'd placed the poem squarely in the Banff-Lake Louise area, but I was drawing many details from memories of climbs elsewhere. I had to be careful these details would stand up to scrutiny from readers whose knowledge of the Rockies and/or mountaineering was much greater than mine. Yet I wasn't trying for a mere piece of regionalism, any more than for a piece of phony melodrama, where the perils are exaggerated, the actions improbable, and the characters mere abstractions.

So, on the one hand, I preserved the names of certain Banff mountains,[2] but, on the other, moved them all closer together in the interests of the unities of time and place, and invented completely my climactic mountain in order to stage the accident exactly. What a recent critic called "the poetic ordering of the landscape"[3] was more important to me than any routine depiction of scenery; a story has its own laws, which the reader doesn't question so long as his sense of the probable isn't violated. I had to watch that I chose the right strata and qualities of rock in the right places (for example, Cambrian holds

[2] Names retained: Inglismaldie, Assiniboine and the Sawback Range. Climbs on Goat, Temple, Girouard, Edith, Sundance and Aylmer supplied many details for my fictitious Fortress, Rampart and Gleam.

[3] Richard Robillard, *Earle Birney*, New Canadian Library 9, (Toronto: McClelland and Stewart, Ltd., 1971), p. 12. This book is recommended for more detailed study of "David."

the rarest fossils; Banff quartzite is treacherous for holds).[4] As it turned out, I wasn't always careful enough. Kites are falcon-like birds never seen flying in Canada west of Saskatchewan. I'd probably picked up the word from *Hamlet* because I liked it. Twenty years after the poem was first published I rewrote two lines when someone showed me what I really meant was hawks.

Another formal aspect of the poem which developed during its writing was a structural use of images. Some of these, such as the skeleton of the goat, and the crippled robin, devices drawn from my own memories, are there to foreshadow the accident and the choice David will make when he finds himself as doomed as the robin. More extensively, I was careful to place a series of words and images in the first part which suggested vitality, youthfulness, joy, energy (an example is "lengthening coltish muscles") and to counterpose them later with symbols of horror and deadness. The long journey up the Finger is described as seen by the two climbers in a mood of sunshiny adventure and merry daring (see p. 25). At the end, the same details reappear in reverse order, suffused with lonely horror: first the peak (now "wind-devilled"), then the chimney, the shining seracs (now "fanged and blinding") and so on.

Beyond this more cerebral carpentry, however, images more satisfying to me welled up of themselves as the poem grew into shape. Without realizing it, I developed a sequence of metaphors (pointed out later by critics) drawn from oceans, the "alien prairie," and even from outer space, to set mountains and nature against the fleeting lives of men. Similarly, certain words became keys which repeated themselves without my knowledge (for example, "splayed," lines 41 and 106). Some of these worked, others were less happy.

Even the story-line made a twist or two of its own, memory suddenly supplying useful details I hadn't known I knew: a phenomenon familiar to all writers in the heat of creating. Some psychologists have described it as the tapping of the

[4] The first fatal accident to a mountaineer in the Canadian Rockies, Abbott's death on Mount Lefroy, was caused by crumbling quartzite.

31

unconscious, that mysterious central source of the brain's energy, an involuntary search-and-discovery of what may be the primordial images we've inherited from the dawn of pre-humanity. It doesn't, of course, follow that "David" is a great poem, even if it could be shown to contain essential myths and archetypal images of the race. I'm saying only that however negligible my poem is when set against the memorable ones of our language, I did experience, in writing it, a rush of imagic energy and excitement beyond and above my rational control. Certain psychiatrists recognize this as a state experienced by many psychotic patients. As Norman Hirt mentions in *The Psychoanalysis of Creativity*, the act of writing takes on a "compelling visional sensitivity," welding conscious and unconscious existence together, and suspending any sense of time in a burning waking dream. It's a temporary state, fortunately for the poet's hold on legal sanity, but a peculiarly intense one for him, of all artists, since he's the one who relies most perhaps on this welling up of charged images to communicate his deepest emotions.

When that flow dwindles, a merely verbal one may continue, and deceive the poet into thinking he's still writing effectively. Writing is a form of intoxication. There's a euphoric "high"; then next morning the hangover. You look at what you've written and realize the last hour was spent saying it all wrong; the verbal compulsion kept going after the imagic rush slowed down. In my case, I suspect I begin to fail at the point where I lose *any* conscious control of the flow, and what might be poetry becomes automatic rhetoric and cliché. *Total* freedom from discipline is a merely negative state. So it often was with "David." And the scars of my nightly defeats are still visible to me in the poem. However, there came a time, some two months after I "saw" that mountain on Bloor Street, when the poem was finished.

But what did "finishing" mean? It meant simply that I gave up trying to make it better, to write it yet again (after at least three complete rewritings). I ceased struggling to make what I had match the glowing dream I'd started with. I settled for something that was a measure of my own limitations, the point where I could no longer see holes in plot or characterization, or places needing lengthening or shortening, tightening or loosening, or anywhere demanding further heightening of the levels of meaning. The sounds and swayings of the words, when I read the poem again aloud to myself, seemed at last consistent, with the dissonances happening only when I wanted. However much farther other poets might have gone, I'd stopped because I couldn't see beyond.

Now, thirty years later, the descriptions seem to me a little lush and self-conscious, the characters underdeveloped, the brief moments of dialogue a bit wooden, the symbolic under-substance shallow, even trite. But maybe these are simply an old man's inability to appreciate himself-when-young. In any case, I couldn't at that time see any way to remedy such defects, even if I could have admitted them, without frustrating my main purpose.

And that, as I could see now I'd "finished" it, was to tell a story about mountains in which the mountains became a character, a personality against whom two youths deliberately matched themselves. They were young men endowed with that intense sensitivity of youth and its capacity for physical joy. And the story was about how they came to the sudden loss of all those endowments through a sort of *hubris*, an overconfident pride in their ability to win all their challenges of the other character. It was truly the tale of "that day, the last of my youth on the last of our mountains"; though even that ending line was unplanned, came blessedly in the final moments of groping with the ultimate rewrite.

Yet what did it all add up to as a statement? Man cannot live in nature without subservience to nature? Wisdom destroys innocence? "In the midst of life we are in death"? Life can be lived to the full only by risking the loss of it? Or some other bromide? You can reduce all poetry to philosophic cliché, all mine at any rate,[5] but I've long ceased to worry that "David" is vulnerable to this kind of intellectual heckling, and it doesn't seem to have troubled even its harshest critics.

[5] See my *The Creative Writer* (Toronto: Canadian Broadcasting Corporation Publications, 1966), pp. 24 ff.

What has exercised some of them, however, is the so-called mercy killing on which the plot turns. It's there to dramatize how terrible the process of merely being alive could suddenly become for them on the very heels of joy. David, at the moment of his mountaineering triumph, is precipitated into a slow and painful dying, for which the only alternative is a quicker death with the help of his friend. Bob, by the same evil chance, is forced to choose between killing his hero or leaving him to die alone and slowly. This was the real choice, even though David describes it as a decision between death or "a wheelchair."

To introduce the latter concept was probably a mistake. I intended it to sound bitterly ironic coming from David, a way of rejecting Bob's conventionally false hope for his friend's recovery. Both men were sufficiently "knowing in the ways of mountains" to be certain that rescue could not come in time. Many fine human beings have lived useful and intellectually satisfying lives in wheelchairs but David could no more have been saved for that destiny than could his wingbroken robin. Consequently Bob pushed David over to prevent his death being miserable and lingering. As a mercy killing, it was no more than an overdose of morphine to a dying patient. Nevertheless it involved an act which many men would not have had the courage or amorality, or whatever it takes, to make. I was simply asking people to believe that *these two men* would have made it. Reactions by readers over the years have taught me that many could not look at the story that way. They took moral stands according to their own religious preconceptions. Of this, more later.

> *Action is transitory,—a step, a blow,*
> *The motion of a muscle...and in the after-vacancy*
> *We wonder at ourselves like men betrayed:*
> *Suffering is permanent...*
> **William Wordsworth**

So much for the writing down of "David." The real writing, however, wasn't done till I had a version which first satisfied my own ear as I read it aloud alone at night in my office, and later passed the more objective listening of my only captive audience, my wife. I don't remember now but I've no doubt she suggested many small changes, all of which I would have furiously resisted, but some of which I probably made. I suspect that most poets, however old at the game, need at least one such critical ally before they can summon the courage to expose their new child to the cold eye of an editor or the chancy reaction of a public audience. In my beginning days as a poet I needed all the reactions I could get, and so I began my

Search for an Audience

That hunt was at first so unsuccessful that I might have burned the poem, as I had done many others, if a few close friends had not seemed honestly to be moved by it. Chief of these was E. J. Pratt, at that time generally regarded as Canada's leading poet. Although I'm not conscious of any direct influence of Pratt on my work, his example had encouraged me to adventure into the writing of a narrative poem with a Canadian wilderness setting. In addition Pratt, as editor of *Canadian Poetry Magazine*, had already published some of my pre-"David" poems. He praised "David" but said it was too long for his magazine and, anyway, I should be able to publish it in some more prestigious journal that could also pay for it. He suggested the *Atlantic Monthly* or *Harper's*. The first rejected it in a week with a note only slightly patronizing, the second sent a printed rejection slip even faster. Then I made extra copies and tried "David" simultaneously in Canada, the U.S., Britain and Australia. After about six months I had by this means accumulated nine more rejections, made either without given reasons or on the score of length.

Pratt, still loyal but running out of ideas, suggested I might try the *University of Toronto Quarterly* whose editor, E. K. Brown, was a senior colleague of mine, with an office located symbolically over my head in the college cloisters. A few weeks after I mailed it to the *Quarterly*, the poem came back with the most curious letter I had yet received. Professor Brown was "deeply impressed," he found it "fine and moving," he had in fact no adverse comments to make, but "the *Quarterly* has published no verse for many years, and . . . the question is one of general policy"; in any case he was resigning as editor to take a job in the United States and wouldn't want now to shape that policy. "Accordingly," he went on, "I have not mentioned the poem to Woodhouse. You can send it to him directly, not mentioning, of course, that I have seen it." Professor Woodhouse was also a colleague, across the hall from me. I walked "David" over to him. He assured me the *Quarterly's* policies would remain singlemindedly devoted to scholarship, and handed me back my poem intact in its envelope. At least I'd saved time, even if my work had become a state secret. What was coming through to me was that both my colleagues disapproved of members of the English Department diverting their energies from scholarly publication. The latter was an activity which might raise the prestige and salaries of all departmental members, but versifying was not. I realized I was up against the Academic Establishment and was not even surprised when the *Quarterly's* editor shortly afterwards published a long and very patriotic poem by Sir Charles G. D. Roberts. It was all right for Sir Charles. He was no scholar, and would never be on our teaching staff. I was a little startled, however, when Professor Brown, several months later, brought out a special issue of new and hitherto unpublished Canadian poetry for an American journal. It did not include the poem which had so "impressed" him.

How long should a poet go on trying in the face of steady rejections? For myself, so long as I felt sure that worse poems were being published all around me and so long as at least one fellow poet whose own work and judgment I respected believed that I should. Pratt was still that friend and encourager and at his urging I now made up a small selection of my poems with "David" as the lead piece, and sent it to Macmillan of Canada. Pratt telephoned his personal recommendation of the book to the firm's editor-in-chief.

Meanwhile I kept trying "David" itself on more magazines. I mailed it to an American mountaineer who was also an editor.

He wrote that he liked it "very much personally because I like climbing . . . but the form is really too traditional. . . ." How traditional is "too"? I had to bolster my courage by reminding myself that Ezra Pound exploited Provençal lyrics and three thousand-year-old Chinese poetry. I sent the piece to another climber, the poet Kenneth Rexroth of San Francisco. He also enjoyed it personally but "climbers don't like literature that stresses falls" and in any case "forty feet isn't very far to do so much damage." I muttered to myself that people kill themselves slipping in bathtubs, and shoved my love-child out again, this time to *Queen's Quarterly.* "We rarely publish narrative verse," they wrote back. They were, of course, publishing narrative *prose.* I was beginning to realize that magazine editors exert considerable control over literary fashion.

Perhaps the most frustrating rejection came next, from William Knickerbocker, then editor of the prestigious *Sewanee Review*, who wrote that he had read my story "with the keenest pleasure . . . but our poetry is set in 10-point Caslon on a somewhat narrow-width page," and if he broke my lines the magazine wouldn't look good. On the other hand, if he set the poem in smaller type, "we would establish a typographical precedent which would also mar the look of our page. I am therefore reluctantly returning . . ."

I did not really believe that great magazines became great from the look of their pages and I now wrote Dorothy Livesay, then one of the "established" younger poets in Canada, asking if she could use "David" in a new poetry magazine she was helping to edit, *Contemporary Verse.* When it was returned ("there isn't room for any but short poems"), I sent it to J. K. Thomas, founding editor of *New World Illustrated* in Toronto. He phoned me almost at once, saying it was the best Canadian poem he'd ever read. But it was back in the mail in a few days with a note from his secretary; they were both "sorry we can't use it"; no reasons were given. Next came an artistically insulting rejection from the editor of *Poetry* (Chicago), George Dillon. He offered to print the first half (everything before the ascent of the Finger). The rest, he said, was mere melodrama.

At last, in November 1941, Macmillan gave their decision.

They loved my book, and especially the "David" poem, with its "controlled suspense . . . superb climax . . . ," and so on. However — my manuscript was enclosed. Ah, if a writer could publish only the warm letters of rejection, what a reputation he could acquire! Macmillan explained that there was "considerable risk" in publishing any "modern Canadian poet," especially in wartime with the cost of paper rising. They would "not be able to make me an offer this year . . . but would like to see the MS again next spring. . . ."

I went back to the round of the magazines until, several rejections later, I came to my last hope. I had myself been literary editor of a magazine, *The Canadian Forum*, until the beginning of the war, but had shied from submitting my poem to it, for fear it might look like favouritism if they printed it and devastate me if they didn't. But now I pocketed pride and gave "David" to Geoff Andrew, its new literary editor. It was accepted.

One December day, more than a year after I had begun my search for a "public," I came in for tea in the small faculty room of my college and there, signalling from the magazine rack, was the new *Canadian Forum*. I sneaked it into the washroom, found the poem in it and read it through for printer's errors — the automatic first response of an author. There were none. I read it again, in a solitary narcissistic glow, then took it back and slid it into the rack, selected another magazine and from behind its cover watched furtively for my first reader. By luck it was a professor of English who was also Principal of the College, the one man in the world who had total say over my salary, promotion and/or dismissal. I happened to know, having once been his student, that he was a somewhat pious Wasp who was inclined to think nothing really good in poetry had happened since Milton. I waited in misery as the great man flipped the pages, stopped, looked up at me, and in a voice in which astonishment and alarm were scarcely concealed, said: "Birney! You've written a *poem!*" Not knowing what else to say, I mumbled, "It's rather long." He frowned. "So I see. Well," he put the magazine down, "I must read it when I get time." He picked up another journal and I slunk out. I never learned if he found the time.

Gradually, however, others did, and blessedly among them were two men whose reactions helped save me from total distrust of my poem and of myself. Both were writers. The first was Wreford Watson, who had recently come to McMaster University from Edinburgh where he had been a younger member of a circle of Scottish poets that included Edwin Muir and Hugh McDermid. Watson wrote me a letter both perceptive and generous, inviting me to his university to give my first public reading of "David." The satisfaction I'd had from seeing the poem at last in print was nothing compared with this new sense of communication I now experienced, reading it to real people gathered together with the help of a respected fellow craftsman, solely to listen. It's chiefly this kind of relationship, direct and "bardic," that's kept me trying to create poems throughout my life.

The second reader most helpful to me was Professor Pelham Edgar, Jamesian critic and a Toronto man-of-letters. He phoned his friend, Lorne Pierce, then editor of the Ryerson Press, and arranged a meeting for me. Pierce asked me to submit to him the book Macmillan had returned. I did and it was accepted. Through the inevitable delays between acceptance and printing, however, it was June of 1942 before the galley proofs of *David and Other Poems* reached me. I read them in a military hospital while recovering from a training accident, for by now I'd left University College (never to return), entered the Canadian Active Army "for the duration," and was qualifying the hard way to be a lieutenant in the infantry.

Five months later the book was published, the first reviews appeared and I began learning some uncomfortable facts about the North American publishing world. I should have known them long before, but I notice there are still some poets and even more critics and teachers of poetry who are less aware of the economics of poetry than they might be.

In the first place, publishers never expect to do more than break even on the sales of a book of poetry unless it's from a poet of long-established international reputation. In Canada in 1942 the average sale of a new book of poetry *by a Canadian* was less than two hundred copies. If it had a hardbound cover it had to sell at least three hundred just to stay out of the red. Since then the Canadian population has increased, but not the ratio of poetry-buyers to people; that's still less than one to fifty thousand.

Second, on such slim margins publishers cannot afford the same heavy costs of national paid advertising for a book of verse which they will risk on a piece of prose fiction. The traditional slim chapbook of verse is not advertised, and gets publicity only if a Canadian newspaper or journal or the CBC decides to review it. The author is dependent on the whim of the larger city dailies and a few national journals for making the very existence of his book known across four thousand miles of country.

Third, few reviewers for the mass media have any special training or competence for judging poetry. Most are journalists in a hurry, columnists holding their readership by appealing to popular tastes at whatever cost to author or publisher. Some are also sheep, following the lead of the first reviewer, whoever he happens to be. Often a good book of poetry, torpedoed on launching, has been sunk without a trace for years until more leisurely and independent critics have a chance to change public opinion about it.

My first reviewer, William Arthur Deacon, was the literary editor of the most widely read morning paper in Canada, the Toronto *Globe and Mail*. He had a Saturday page in which he made a point of being the earliest anywhere to review a new Canadian book, and Toronto publishers made sure that no one got an advance copy before W.A.D. I was lucky, in my publisher's opinion, that he gave my book a favourable critique. My enthusiasm was tempered, however, when I saw that he virtually ignored "David" to lavish eulogies on the poem which I felt then, and still feel, to be the weakest in the book. It was a piece expressing bitter acceptance of my own need to take part in the war. In its first year World War II had seemed to be only another struggle between imperialisms, but now it was also a final stand to stop Hitler's fascists from destroying all democratic and socialistic societies and any hope of a better world. The critic had exploited this one poem in my book in a

40

spirit of conventional patriotism, and his lead was followed by various provincial journalists. The first printing of five hundred went in a few weeks.

Then a more thoughtful and discriminating reviewer, B. K. Sandwell, editor of *Saturday Night*, turned the emphasis onto the "David" poem, and the combination of his judgment and the early sales roused a New York publisher to wire for a copy. Selling five hundred copies was scarcely a literary conquest, however; especially since at least a hundred of those had been given away either by the publisher for public relations, or by me for my private ones, to friends and to other poets who couldn't or wouldn't pay the dollar and a half it cost. I heard nothing more from the New York publisher, and my own, caught by surprise, failed to get a second printing into the bookstores until Christmas was past and the chance of "gift sales" had vanished.

Then came the inevitably cooler critical assessment by later reviewers. The CBC rejected my proposal to read "David" over radio, and though they allowed an appreciative teacher to do it for me, they also paid another educationalist to blast the poem over national airwaves for its "lack of rhyme and straining toward primitive Canadianism," whatever that meant.

But most readers remained kind, even some whose praise was not predictable. There was an enthusiastic letter from Sir Charles G. D. Roberts and further radio broadcasts of "David," now by professional actors, notably Lister Sinclair and Arthur Hill, whose interpretations helped me greatly in my own later readings of the poem.

In Great Britain and the United States, however, twenty review copies disappeared without leaving a review behind. There was a war on, of course, and it was at that time still going badly for our side. In any case, why review a book in London or New York that couldn't be bought anywhere except in Canada? Why be interested in the produce of a colonial publisher who made no effort to export? And when a second printing appeared in Toronto and the title poem was reprinted in A. J. M. Smith's *The Book of Canadian Poetry* (1943), an anthology with U.S. and British outlets, the English and

American publishers lost all interest in my book since they "could no longer count on sales either in Canada or elsewhere."

Even at home I found, as most Canadian authors must, that getting a hardcover book published, tricky as that may be, isn't as difficult as persuading booksellers, other than the leading half dozen in the whole country, to stock it. My Hamilton poet friend, Wreford Watson, wrote me that he'd been required by his bookseller to pay in advance for the copy he ordered, and when he arrived to claim it he was asked if he wouldn't prefer the new American reprint of Robert W. Service which had just come in.

The second printing was "exhausted," as they say, by April 1943 but by then, so also was my publisher's interest. He decided not to republish, even when the book received the Governor-General's Award, because, as he later confessed to me, he knew I'd be sent overseas and he wasn't sure if I'd ever come back to write another.

What had mainly deterred the foreign publishers, I think, was that they could not control anthology and broadcast rights. These are almost the only sources of continued revenue for a poem, and are usually held jointly by the original publisher and the poet. Thus from the sales of the two printings of the book, *David and Other Poems*, I netted less than $50.00, even assuming my time as valueless, and not counting income tax which I was then too poor to pay anyway. The original appearance of "David" in *The Canadian Forum* had been gratis, but from anthology rights for the poem, which gradually rose from $15.00 in 1945 to $250.00 today, my publishers and I have together received about $3500.00. The editors of the anthologies themselves have done even better out of it. These mercenary details are mentioned in the interests of a realistic approach to the study of Canadian literature.

Much more important to me was the growth of a single poem's audience. It started with my wife and a few friends, and grew through the few hundred readers of *The Canadian Forum*, the almost thousand buyers and many thousand library borrowers of the printed book, to the post-war listeners on national radio and the hundreds of thousands of students reading it in high school and university texts across Canada and, recently, in the United States.

"David" became, in fact, a captive of Education and at one time or another was assigned reading in schools or colleges of all the provinces, at any level between grade eight and graduate seminars in "Can. Lit." In Quebec, however, it's read only in the English-speaking schools, nor has it ever been translated into French or any other language, to my knowledge, except German.

It was, on the other hand, given what I like to think of as the ultimate flattery — a full-length parody, forty stanzas plus footnotes, by a very bright high school senior. He retitled the story "Saul" and retold it with the switch that the hero now *wants* to be saved for a wheelchair; any way that he can stay alive is okay by him. But Bobby insists Saul will be happier if pushed over and proceeds vigorously to the task. I'm sorry "Saul" isn't better known, but at least it gained Tom Franck, its author, the admittance he sought to a poetry writing workshop that I used to referee at the University of British Columbia. He reacted to that experience by switching to law and is now a distinguished Professor of International Jurisprudence somewhere in the United States.

The adoption of "David" by schools and colleges made it increasingly easier for me to find youthful audiences to whom I could read this and other poems of mine. Making the rounds of British Columbia high schools in the late forties brought me into exciting contact with a larger cross-section of students than I was getting in my classes at U.B.C. In the fifties, I read the poem to university audiences in other parts of Canada; one June day in 1952 I had the special pleasure of sounding it to a national gathering of librarians on the ski slopes of Mount Norquay, looking out over Banff toward Inglismaldie and other peaks of the poem. By some freak of the P.A. system and the contours of the ski slopes, my voice funnelled down amplified into the ears of startled citizens on Banff's main street. For nearly all of them it was surely their one and only contact with the poem. But later it was put on the Alberta school curriculum and knowledge of it became enforced. This, in turn, led to my revisiting Banff recently to read "David" in the town's beautiful new arts centre, while a professional photographer, Don Beers, who is also a high school English teacher and has memorized the poem, kept pace with colour slides matching, line by line, its details and images of nature. That was the ultimate, for me, in reaching out with this poem to other people's consciousnesses.

I've no desire ever to read it again. In the twenty years between the two readings in Banff, I've moved into other modes and ways of writing; the composing of it had been an act out of "the last of my youth" too, and sometimes "David" seems to stand in the way of later and better work. For me, it belongs back in the forties in which it was written and best enjoyed. Yet the reading and study of it by others continues, and perforce my concern that it should be read, not out of duty and in literalmindedness, but as a free act, a sharing in the pleasures of the uninhibited imagination. And this is what the rest of the book is about — about processes in reading poetry, about reading poetry in general, and first of all about *uncreative* ways of reading "David."

2 READING POETRY

Writing "David" and finding readers and listeners for it were matters over which I had some say. Now I'm talking about happenings over which I've had little control: the interpretation, apprehension and, above all, the various "teachings" of the poem.

First I'll try to dramatize how varied these can be by inventing a dialogue. If it seems to bring out mainly the worst in teaching, have patience. Later I'll shift to emphasize the positive. But for the moment let's pretend I've come to a high school on the invitation of two teachers, Miss Gudgeon and Mr. Stemm, who've been enterprising enough to write me that they each had a class in which they were going to "take up" my poem and they wanted my advice before starting. I've replied, agreeing to join them if they'd include in our meeting a student representative from each class. They've consented, though Mr. Stemm showed rather modified enthusiasm. So here I am. I meet the students, Eileen and Tom, and after the usual politenesses we get down to

A. Dialogue of Five about

Unhearing

MISS G:
Where do we begin?

ME:
I hope none of you has read the poem.

MISS G:
Oh, but of course we've *all* read it! We've done that at least!

ME:
Out loud? (Silence) Or on recording?

EILEEN:
Why don't you read it to us now?

TOM:
Hey right!

MISS G:
I'm sure we all want to hear you read it but we do have to be out of this room (looking at her watch) when the lunch bell rings at 11:57.

ME:
(Looking out at a sunny slope of grass) It's a fine warm September day. The lawn looks dry. Would you all like to bring your lunches out later? I could read while you eat. It takes fourteen minutes.

TOM:
Great.

EILEEN:
Can I bring a friend?

ME:
I hope your lawns are for everybody. Guitarists especially welcome to strum along.

MR. S:
(Astonished) You will *sing* it?!

ME:
No, but I would if I could, and it does have a regular downbeat and other repeated cadences. That's one reason I wanted you to hear it sounded before anything else.

MR. S:
You don't believe poetry must come to us first on the page?

ME:
No longer. Not with sound tapes, disks, cassettes and videotapes available, and the quality so greatly improved. Now you can get the more prominent living poets speaking their own stuff, and lots of earlier verse read by leading actors.

MR. S:
Yes, this is all very helpful, but I still think we have to have the text of anything first to know what we're getting. Don't you think students prefer it that way?

MISS G:

It *is* hard to follow a strange poem just by ear.

ME:

Do you agree, Tom?

TOM:

Depends what you mean by poetry. What about Simon and Garfunkel, or Joan Baez? Millions of kids know their songs and lots of them haven't ever seen the words written down!

EILEEN:

Sure, and what about Bob Dylan or John Lennon? People heard them first on records.

ME:

Absolutely! We shouldn't get trapped into any definitions of poetry that exclude such artists, or the best folk songs, whether new or old. Where there's a happy get-together of words and images and emotions and rhythms, there's poetry, in my book, whether it's "the cow jumped over the moon" or "Absent thee from felicity awhile . . ." Besides, I don't think we expect to follow any new piece of creation effortlessly the first time. Miss G, you listen to symphonic records. What contemporary composers do you like? John Cage?

MISS G:

No, I don't understand him at all. Stravinsky, I guess — yes, I see what you mean. I didn't like him at first either, but —

ME:

But "David" isn't in his class. I know it isn't! My point is only that a poem is also in its limited way music, a harmony of the sound of words, or their phonemes. But that music can die unnoticed, if the listener too quickly involves himself in the unravelling of "meaning" and "symbolism" and other intellectualities. That's why I want the sound of a poem to get its innings at the start of a student's acquaintance with it.

TOM:

(Groans) Not de-dum-de-dum?! Iambics, bla-bla. Sorry, Mr. Birney, but all that really turns me off.

ME:
That isn't really what I mean, Tom. That's just the dry bones of the poem clacking. What's important are the variations, the breaks, the style of the poem, just as in a good combo. Any effective speaker of poetry knows this.

MISS G:
But *is* the poet a good speaker of his poem?

ME:
Touché. Too often not. But it's *his* voice the poem is programmed to. He's notated it, and so he has some authority on the sounding of it, whether or not he's a virtuoso.

TOM:
Got it. Like when a composer plays his own music it won't be so hot maybe as Glenn Gould or Rubenstein doing it, but he'll have the rhythm the way he wants.

EILEEN:
Right. It's his vibes in the first place and you tune in on them.

MR. S:
Perhaps we'd better get back to "David" before the bell rings.

ME:
Okay. So this time, we've read it before we've heard it. What text are you using? . . . Hmm. Yes, I see. What about these footnotes? Do you read them, Tom?

TOM:
Exam insurance.

EILEEN:
Well, I really need them.

ME:
Eileen, did you learn anything about the poem's metre and rhyme from them?

EILEEN:
Oh yes. It's iambic pentameter. And it's unrhymed — blank verse.

ME:
Sorry. Never believe anything just because it's in print. (I speak

the first stanza and together we work out the basic sound-patterns by spot-checking through the poem.) Okay. Footnote writers sometimes don't read the poem out loud either, or they're dull in the inner ear.

MR. S:

You're right, of course. There's regular assonantal rhyme, and it's not iambic. But do you know, Mr. Birney, that Dr. Desmond Pacey, in his book *Creative Writing in Canada,* describes "David" as a blank verse poem? I believe he was a well-known English Professor and is now a University Vice-President.

ME:

Yes. We've just proved that even VIPs make mistakes, lapse into

Unreading

Unfortunately, some footnote writers perpetuate the lapses. In fact, that error is repeated in Coles' *Notes* for "David," a crib once relied on by thousands of grade 13 students in Ontario.

TOM:

Wow! I've got a second-hand copy of that in my room now! I was going to use it for the exam. Are there any other boobs?

ME:

Including printing errors there are about eighty, by my count. I'll lend you my corrected copy.

EILEEN:

But does everybody have to have the same opinion about your poem that you do?

ME:

It was time somebody asked that. Of course not! A good question, I want to answer it in a moment. But right now I'm not talking about literary judgments, only about technical facts. Contrary to Coles' *Notes,* it's a fact that the pika mentioned in "David" is not a fish, and its slicing pipe is not "the cry of a pike . . . in the mountain streams," nor is it something "like a rabbit" as the same source says a few pages later. Even the condensed *Webster's Collegiate* tells us the pika is a rat-like rodent; it inhabits mountain scree, and its peculiar piping cry is the chief evidence of its presence. Scree, moreover, is not "a gulley" but a fan of loose rock weathering down from a cliff; since the heavier boulders roll farther, the fan begins with rock dust and shale before coarsening into gravel; consequently a descending alpinist can make fantastic speed loping down the higher scree.[1]

MR. S:
Surely some footnotes are useful.

ME:
What do you students think?

EILEEN:
Gee, ours just tell me what any dumb cluck knows already, like for "the wail of mosquitoes" we got a note saying "the drone of mosquitoes."

TOM:
Yeah, and there aren't any notes for the real tricky things.

ME:
Like what?

TOM:
Like "beetle-seal in the rock." I looked up my Coles' *Notes* on that one and it says "a beetle has been pressed into the rock" but you're talking about a trilobite, aren't you, and that's not a beetle. Besides, it was sealed into mud that *became* rock. I've had enough geology to know that.

ME:
Check! It depends on the poem. Footnotes have value for Eliot's *The Waste Land*, I suppose — since Eliot himself felt it necessary to supply some. But I think "David" is basically a simple poem, and whatever subtleties it may have will become understandable with two or three readings (especially if one of them's oral), and a little imagining. When I read other people's poems I *enjoy* sounding, re-reading, and thinking about them.

1 For further corrections of Coles' and other notes, see Appendix B.

MISS G:

But many of your readers have never been in mountains, and most of them aren't mountaineers.

ME:

Right! So for a complete verbal understanding they'd have to look up maybe a dozen words in their personal dictionary, to indulge in a little self-teaching. But why not? Using a dictionary is fun, if you like words at all, more fun than bad footnotes. And more accurate than relying on what could only be called

Unteaching

TOM:

But suppose you don't like words all that much? We're not all poets.

ME:

Tom has a point. I didn't write "David" to help people improve their vocabulary. If a reader finds it boring to pin down the meanings of every word, he should stop trying.

EILEEN:

But what if you have to produce an essay about it? Or make a paraphrase or something?

ME:

I didn't write the poem to provide material for examination torture, or essay topics, or paraphrases. No poet ever does. In fact, I deplore these practices as perversions of art, which is made to be enjoyed, and as unteaching. You should be allowed to find your own creative reaction to the poem. Parapaint it if you like to paint, or become aware of how "David" makes you *feel*, and sculpt or sing it.

MR. S:

You don't think we should teach your poem at all then?

ME:

I don't think poetry can be "taught" except by being enjoyed. By forced labour, no. The poem was born in a kind of ecstasy, as well as agony. If it's any good, it can transmit something of the ecstasy *without* the agony. But the listener or reader must approach it in the same spirit of giving birth. A poem is a creative writing and experiencing; it can also be creative reading. *It's the uncreative reader I want less of* — the plodding footnoter, the essay-trapped student, the unimaginative critic, the over-rational academic, the literal-minded teacher. I — (Bell rings) Oh no!

TOM:
We're just getting started.

EILEEN:
Can't we carry this on at lunch when you read the poem?

MR. S:
I am afraid I'll have uncreative duties for the rest of the day. Miss G?

MISS G:
I have a free hour after lunch. I'll stay.

ME:
Great! Let's expand the dialogue to as many as possible.

B. Dialogue of Many about

Uncreative Reading

(On the lawn, after sounding the poem; Miss G, Eileen, several students and a few teachers who've joined us.)

ME:
We were talking about the uncreative approach to creativity. How has it got established? Well, maybe it starts with the journalistic book-reviewers, more interested in gossiping about the poet than understanding his poems. Then, it's carried on by lazy textbook makers and sloppy study methods in schools. I'll give you examples. There was a critic who, simply because I'd been at college with him in Vancouver, told his readers that "David" takes place in the Coast Range; that's five hundred miles in the wrong direction, wrong province, wrong scenery. Another "authority," a professor who knew I'd had my

high schooling in the Kootenays, informed everybody that "David" is set in the Crow's Nest Pass — again, hundreds of miles off, where the mountains aren't even glaciated. Then a university student from Toronto, confronted with the contradictory authorities, wrote to ask me which one was right. If he (or his two information experts) had turned to the nearest atlas and looked up Mount Assiniboine, he and I would have been saved the time, stamps and energy of correspondence.

MISS G:
But surely that student showed initiative.

ME:
Yes, but not in ducking his own homework when his professors flunked on theirs.

MISS G:
Well, I could do with more students who read something and then do something about it.

ME:
What do the rest of you think? Should he have written me?

TALL STUDENT:
You're the one who knows. So he went to you.

SHORT STUDENT:
Yeah, but if we all wrote him, he wouldn't have time to answer anybody or do any more writing himself.

ME:
Maybe you're both right, but I do answer at least 95 percent of student mail. I only wish it was all useful to the senders or fun for me. Instead, most of it tells me something's gone wrong back at the farm. Nobody seems to make use of good source material. However dull or confusing a student may find "David" itself, he can easily vivify it by turning to illustrations of the Canadian Rockies available in standard reference books, film shorts, colour slides, or whatever. In the universities, of course, there is much more information of this sort available about famous climbs and climbers, the wild life and so forth. Yet I've never seen any of the numerous professorial footnoters

53

referring students to even the basic reference books on climbing in the Rockies.[2]

TALL STUDENT:

What about film material? We've got too many books to read already.

ME:

Yes, I wish all schools today budgeted more towards the acquisition of educational TV, tapes and films. Field trips into the Rockies would be the best supplement, of course, but that's only feasible for students in some parts of Alberta and British Columbia. But there's plenty of visual material and there's also often a chance to hear and see travelogues by live speakers — travellers, climbers, poets and so on — which would greatly broaden anybody's understanding of our mountains.

OLDER TEACHER (MALE):

I'm all for this but I wish you poets appreciated how little time we have to plan such things, even if we were given the money to do it.

ME:

I can guess. I was an overworked and underbudgeted prof most of my life. But some teachers manage better than others on the same resources. I remember getting a letter from one in Fergus, Ontario, who was gradually putting together a complete collection of films and book photos to illustrate the mountain background of "David," simply for classroom purposes. She sent me a list of what she had and asked me to suggest other source material. That's the kind of letter I'm very happy to answer. Then there's Don Beers, the Calgary teacher who over several years has put together a collection of his own colour slides to illustrate "David" line by line. He took his

[2] eg., H. R. Belyea, *The Story of the Mountains; Banff National Park*. Geological Survey of Canada (Ottawa: Department of Mines and Technical Surveys, 1960). *The Canadian Alpine Journal*, 1915 to present.

James Outram, *In the Heart of the Canadian Rockies* (London, New York: Macmillan, 1948).

Frank S. Smythe, *Rocky Mountains* (London: Black, 1948). For views of Mount Assiniboine, see pp. 96-100, 103; see also *Climbs in the Canadian Rockies* (London: Hoddart/Stoughton, 1950).

holidays in the mountains to do it, made his own photographs, and ended up not only with a show the students really grooved on, but as a professional photographer.

YOUNG TEACHER:

I must buy a camera!

ME:

Well, there are dozens of Canadian poets who'd enjoy collaboration with photographers and painters.

MISS G:

I would think a poet would find it limited his poem too much to have it illustrated.

ME:

For myself, only if it's poorly done; technically, I mean. I'm always excited when a visual artist is triggered to remake something I've written. It hasn't happened often; only once with "David" within book covers. Leonard Brooks transformed one line — "Stairs from the valley, and steps to the sun's retreats" — into a whole visual trip for me in his illustrations to my *Selected Poems*. On the other hand, some good artists doing routine "jobs" for publishers or magazine editors can be liabilities to the writer. When I got the first proof for the title page of *David and Other Poems* I found I was up against a drawing by someone who seemingly had never been west of Toronto. He drew my Finger looking like some tired old Laurentian hill you could have rolled all the way down without hurting anything but your self-respect. I had to redraw it to prevent my readers referring vainly to it for the overhangs, ledges, chimneys, glaciers, cirques and all the other details of real mountains integral to the poem.

YOUNG TEACHER:

So you drew the Finger from your memory of the real mountain?

ME:

No, I drew it from the description in the poem.

EILEEN:

But isn't that the same thing?

ME:

There was no "real" mountain. First I invented a story, then a mountain to fit it.

ANOTHER YOUNG TEACHER:

But there *is* such a mountain. There's a Mount Finger. And it's in the Sawback Range west of Banff, right where you put it. I know because I met a man who climbed it years ago.

ME:

Right. There is now, but that mountain was unnamed until after "David" appeared.

ANOTHER YOUNG TEACHER:

Nuts! This man found David's cairn on the top. And I've seen the peak myself. Anybody can, driving along the new Trans-Canada Highway. There's even a sign pointing to it.

ME:

That's right. That highway was also created after the poem was published, and so was the sign.

ANOTHER YOUNG TEACHER:

Ah, but I've seen the drawing on the title page of your book and *it's just like this mountain.* What gives?

ME:

Sure, it looks a bit like the one I drew thirty years ago, but Mount Finger didn't have any name until as late as 1955, and was still unnamed on the Department of Mines and Technical Surveys' Map of 1959. When that Fergus, Ontario teacher I was talking about complained to me that she'd examined all the official maps showing the Sawback Range and there was no Finger marked on it, I told her the Sawback was full of aiguilles shaped much like a fist with a pointing index finger; that's why I placed my imaginary mountain in that particular range.

ANOTHER YOUNG TEACHER:

(Still unconvinced) Well, I don't know. My mountaineer friend said he wasn't the first to climb it. There was even an earlier ascent written up in the *Canadian Alpine Journal.*

ME:

Your friend is correct. Two expert mountaineers reported having made an ascent in 1956 of a Mount Finger on the Sawback. They photographed the mountain and drew charts of their route. These were included in their account of the climb.[3]

ANOTHER YOUNG TEACHER:

Well, so the mountain *does* exist.

ME:

Sure, for some millions of years. The earliest recorded climb was by the Swiss guide, Lawrence Grassi, in the 1930s. He built the first cairn. But the peak was named long afterwards by people, not necessarily climbers, who thought it looked like the Finger in my poem.

ANOTHER YOUNG TEACHER:

So how come you put your Finger in the Sawback Range and drew it to look like a mountain actually there, even if it wasn't named anything yet?

ME:

A damned good question. The answer puzzled me for a while. But the last time I was driving up from Banff to Lake Louise it hit me. In the 1920s I did scramble up to a big sheep cave called the Hole-in-the-Wall, on the sheer of another peak in the same range. Now I realize that when I reached that cave's mouth, I'd have glimpsed the peak now called the Finger from an angle that makes it look strikingly finger-like. I don't *remember* seeing it, but I do recall now that the nearest I've come to a climber's death was a few minutes later that day. I started to descend by a different route by jumping on some loose scree below the cave. That started a small rockslide which gripped and carried me to within a few feet of the edge of the sheer, with at least a five hundred-foot drop straight below, before I could scramble onto solid rock. I think now that in my subconscious I filed away both memories — of the

---

[3] See H. Gmoser and Ken Baker, "Mount Finger," *Canadian Alpine Journal,* XL (1957), 84-85. They found goats, a "chimney," rotten ridge-rock and a broken cairn on the peak, but their account makes no reference to the poem.

fingerish peak and of my narrow escape — and both broke
surface together when I was writing "David."

ANOTHER YOUNG TEACHER:
I can buy that. But it doesn't explain why my friend came on a
dead goat at the bottom of the Finger in 1962 or why, to make
the peak, he had to find a chimney and climb eighty feet up to
the summit. And he found rotting rock on the top too.[4]

ME:
Nothing marvellous about all that. There are goats on those
mountains, or there were in my generation, all mortal. And
nearly every peak on the Sawback is likely to have a vertical
fracture wide enough to be called a chimney. There's brittle
rock on those serrations, Devonian limestone and quartzite,
which has suffered what the geologists call extreme crustal
shortening.

ANOTHER YOUNG TEACHER:
Well, I still think it's weird. Everybody I know believes it all
happened to you.

ME:
You mean I got shoved off a cliff?

YOUNG TEACHER:
Maybe you did the shoving!

MISS G:
Oh please, Mr. Birney has had enough of this, I'm sure. We've
got off the subject.

ME:
No, I suspect we're still talking about Uncreative Reading, and
one of its by-products,

---

[4] See Karl Ricker & Ann Morton, "How many routes on the 'Finger'?" *Canadian
Alpine Journal*, XLVI (1963), 88-95; also I. Stirling "The Finger of Sawback,"
Varsity Outdoor Club Journal (U.B.C.),IV (1961), 36. Ricker and Morton's
article begins: "Modern legend, based on a poem written by Dr. Earle Birney,
has led at least ten climbing parties in the last few years to an intriguing rock
climb near Banff. It is not known whether the hero in "David" actually
climbed the spire. . ." (Note the assumption that David was a real
mountaineer.)

Uncreative Teaching

OTHER TEACHER:
Oh oh! You're after us teachers again!

ME:
Not really, but nearly all of us have trouble keeping myth and reality separate, myself included.

OTHER TEACHER:
How do you mean?

ME:
I mean, as I said before, that "David" is a piece of fiction. Some of it came out of personal experience, some out of my imaginings. This mixing of fact and fancy doesn't bother me so long as I can fuse the two and make the fantasy part seem so real that the reader accepts the whole as true for the time he's reading it. Ever since Aristotle, we've been accustomed to the idea that readers or listeners can be persuaded to suspend temporarily their natural tendency not to believe something "made-up." It's when they *permanently* accept fiction as fact that I must reassert my own identity as the maker of my fiction, not as a character in it.

MISS G:
But isn't it your responsibility as the artist if readers get permanently confused?

ME:
On the contrary. "David" is plainly published and circulated as a narrative poem, a fiction, not an autobiography.

TOM:
But you tell it in the first person.

ME:
Browning told "Childe Roland to the Dark Tower Came" and "My Last Duchess" in the first person but he was a nineteenth century Englishman, not a medieval knight or the Duke of Ferrara. Herman Melville was neither Ishmael nor Moby Dick, and Defoe stayed home and imagined himself Robinson Crusoe.

TOM:

So what use is this "first person" stuff?

ME:

The "first person" is a device to create the illusion of reality. It's a natural one, especially for poets and symbolic novelists. First, it's the basic "I" of lyrical poetry in which no one, not even the poet, will ever know how much of it is himself and how much is someone else. Second, it's essential in dramatic monologue. In fact, the use of an "I," a persona, is the simplest, most fundamental convention of poetry. Only small children or adults totally unsophisticated in literature could really be confused by it.[5] If students graduate from high schools and even from universities, still unable to appreciate and enjoy the difference between a piece of writing that asks them to indulge their imagination and a piece that is trying to report literally something that actually happened, then there's something wrong with their education. Their minds have become so prosaic that they can no longer imagine an imagining; they have to make it into a "reportage." As John Stuart Mill said, "Originality is the one thing which unoriginal minds cannot feel the use of."

Not pickt from the leaves of any author, but bred amongst the weeds & tares of my own brain.
                                    Sir Thomas Browne

TOM:

But maybe it's just in the Rockies where the scene is laid that you get readers seeing it as "really real"?

ME:

Wish I could agree, Tom, but judging from several hundred letters sent me over the last twenty-five years by both students

[5] See Louis Dudek, *The First Person in Literature* (Toronto: Canadian Broadcasting Corporation Publications, 1967).

60

and teachers of "David" (as well as of other poems of mine), I'd say the literal approach is a national educational hang-up. I've brought some of those letters, by the way. Is there time to read extracts?[6]

MISS G:

(Looking at her watch) You've got about twenty-three minutes before the next bell.

ME:

Okay. Here's one from an Ontario girl in grade 13: "Is the story of 'David' true? My English teacher was uncertain and suggested someone find out, so I took it upon myself to write you. Is 'David' based on true fact, hearsay, a newspaper article, or a figment of the imagination, or what? I would appreciate an answer to this as quick as possible."

MISS G:

Well, it's a form of flattery. You should feel complimented.

ME:

Not really. I'm sure the girl who wrote me that was alert, enterprising, efficient. But what if every student of "David," or even ten percent of them, did that? I'd have to employ a secretary and ask for a Canada Council grant just to tell well-meaning students (and teachers) that fiction is a stew of facts, hearsay, news articles and "figments," and that any reader who tries to separate the carrots from the rest of the stew sets himself a hopeless, irrelevant, meaningless task. Also a destructive task, because meantime the food gets cold.

OTHER TEACHER:

But is a poem something to eat?

ME:

Yes! It was made to be tasted, eaten if liked, ingested and turned into nourishment, into soul food. It's not an excuse for students to practise journalistic intrusions into the private life of an author. If a story seems "true" to you, let it be "true," let it be.

[6] For more extracts, see Appendix A.

OTHER TEACHER:
But you can't expect people to know for sure whether stories are true or not.

ME:
Okay. But why should they? My point is that students who find a piece of fiction "real" should be encouraged to enjoy the illusion, and turn their research drives into studying *how* the poem creates that sense of reality.

TOM:
More examples? You said it was an all-Canadian habit, this not accepting a story for its own sake.

ME:
Yes. Here's a grade 11 student in Manitoba: "Is this poem true? If not, where on earth did the idea come from?" Now I feel quite sure no Canadian student would write a British or American author in that tone. Underneath, I suspect, is an assumption that real imaginative literature is created only in other countries and imported by us, and that Canadians write only about what actually happens to them.

YOUNG TEACHER:
Aren't you being unduly sensitive about this? As a teacher I'd encourage students to write even Robert Graves in Majorca, or Jorge Borges wherever he might happen to be, if I knew the address and thought they'd get an answer.

ME:
You might get a rude one if you asked them "how on earth" they could have imagined something.

YOUNG TEACHER:
But no one invents out of nothing. Alexander Graham Bell was a great Canadian inventor but he needed electricity and some wire and several previously discovered facts about the physics of sound before he could invent the telephone.

ME:
Agreed! There's always a tradition, and a medium, and a basis of experience in creating anything. But you don't have to dissect a telephone to enjoy using it. What's important to the

62

reader of a poem is its enjoyment. Unless the student wants to be a literary critic — and that's maybe one in a thousand in high school classes — dissecting and detecting and source-hunting in poems is probably going to kill his interest in it *as a work of the imagination.* Consider, for example, the plight of this grade 12 girl: "I can't understand where the Finger is located," she writes me, all the way from rural Nova Scotia. All her classmates have different ideas, she says. Will I please settle the matter? I'll have to tell her it's in the Rock Candy Mountains, in the Dominion of No Sense, which is divided into Five Senses, none sensible and all contained in a Sixth.

Look, I wrote a short story in verse to transmit excitement, communicate emotion, meditate on experience, imagine strangeness. Don't reduce it to a route map of the Sawback Range. A poem is an art object.

ANOTHER STUDENT:
Weren't you also trying to write propaganda?

ME:
Propaganda? Whatever for?

ANOTHER STUDENT:
Well, for mercy killing, for one thing.

ME:
Oh Lord, this is the biggest misconception of the lot!

ANOTHER STUDENT:
Well, there *is* a mercy killing in it.

ME:
Sure. You could also say the poem teaches people to stay in the valley and play poker.

YOUNG TEACHER:
I agree it's bad teaching if students come out of "David" assuming it's a simple autobiography and a moral tract for euthanasia but students don't take poetry *that* literally.

ME:
Don't kid yourself. Two U.B.C. colleagues of mine told me

they actually overheard one freshman during fall registration say to another:

"I'm really gonna be sunk in English. You know whose section they put me in?"

"No. Whose?"

"Birney's."

"Who's he?"

"The guy that wrote 'David'."

"David, who's he?"

"Yuh dope. It's a poem, yuh had it in grade 10. He's the sonofabitch who pushed his best friend offen a cliff."

"Jeez, you better git a transfer."

STILL ANOTHER STUDENT:
Yeah, that's a laugh, but those prof pals of yours were just having you on!

ME:
Maybe. That was back in 1946, and I didn't hear the students with my own ears. But in 1971 I saw with my own eyes the following statement in an essay on Canadian poetry by an English professor at the University of Alberta: "It is true that 'David' conforms closely to the narrative style, but there is proof that this was no imaginary story. Birney's companion on that fatal mountain climb was a *real* David. His death was reported as being due to a rockslide."[7]

STILL ANOTHER STUDENT:
Wow! This prof's got proof! So how come you keep saying you made up the story?

ME:
Because the professor has made up *her* story. She has no proof, doesn't even try to offer any. Worse, she is herself a poet and deep down must know better.

YOUNG TEACHER:
That's really far out! But so what? No proof! In the long run that sort of wild remark gets forgotten.

[7] Dorothy Livesay, "The Documentary Poem: A Canadian Genre," *Contexts of Canadian Criticism*, ed. Eli Mandel (Chicago: University of Chicago Press, 1972), p. 279.

ME:

Maybe. But not in the short run. When a professor broadcasts such nonsense, how can students keep from being confused about the very nature of poetry and the nature of poets? For the implication is that I in fact pushed "a real David" over a cliff and am still legally a murderer outwitting justice by a false report about "a rockslide"! I don't wonder therefore that when I give readings in schools or university auditoriums, even if I avoid reading "David" at all, the first question likely to be asked me at the end is "Did the story in 'David' really happen to you?" For some, it seems the only question that interests them, and they're disappointed, even bewildered, that I don't answer with a simple "Yes."

TOM:

Ah, students have got to think of something to ask, or write you, if the teacher told them to.

STILL ANOTHER TEACHER:

That's also one way to get your autograph, you know.

ME:

Check. They don't write Wordsworth only because they know he's dead. Okay. But what's really bothering me is that behind some of these letters I feel the lingering presence of the old Authoritarian Teaching.

OTHER TEACHER:

You're out of date! That's long dead.

ME:

Is it? Essays still *have* to be written. The poem says so-and-so: true or false? The story sounds real — maybe it is. Make sure; write Birney and *get the facts.* Memorize these stanzas. Do this and that or you'll fail.

OTHER TEACHER:

You're shooting at the wrong target, Mr. Birney. It's the universities that keep the pass-fail system going. The whole trend in the schools now is against numerically graded essays and quizzes, against exams, against single-text authority and authoritarian teaching.

ME:

Apologies. The last few years have seen great changes, I know. Yet it's only a year or so ago that John Young, the Principal of a British Columbia high school, was quoted as saying — let me get it exact, I have the clipping here — that "our schools are still slaves to the timetable, the teacher-dominated lesson, the control and suppression of ideas, and the suppression of the excitement, spontaneity and joy of learning."[8] I doubt if he is all wrong.

TOM:

He's got a point or two anyway. My kid brother in grade 8 is stuck with memorizing poems he hates just because the teacher makes him; all his class has to, and they get marks off for every mistake they make in recitation.

ME:

Yes, I've been reading an article only a few months old which uses this kind of example to protest against our present educative process generally, as one which is "teaching us all to see the same world" and see it "the same way."[9]

EILEEN:

But the world *is* the same now; it *is* a global village. People have to give up all their different set ways and learn to live in peace together.

ME:

What you say is true; we can't know too much about others, and the big world outside our parish. But we don't have to become computerized robots in the process. In fact, we can only make progress in understanding if we at the same time develop further understanding of ourselves. Education has got to help us explore inwards as well as outwards.

TOM:

I buy that. Maybe now you're getting down to something posi-

---

[8] Robert McKeown, "Is your School Obsolete?" *Weekend Magazine* (12 Sept., 1970), p. 4.
[9] Morris Wolfe, "The Case against 'Education'," *Saturday Night* (August 1971), pp. 29-30.

tive. You're saying poems should be studied to find out about yourself.

ME:

That's pretty close to what I mean. Let's throw out "studied," and just say "experienced." Poems are written personally and offered for enjoyment the same way; finding the one pre-supposed theme, the "right" symbols, and arriving at the same "understanding" and value-judgment (if any) by Christmas does not make for an individual experience.

EILEEN:

But shouldn't a good poem offer values for society in general?

ME:

It does. Great poems, like great music, enrich the lives of people by expanding their inner consciousness and intensifying their appreciation of life, their love of being alive. The arts have that kind of value. They don't operate either to reconcile us to whatever kind of society we are born into, or to stream-line us into global think-alikes. I certainly don't write anything, poems or whatever, to make people loyal and accepting of the present society of Western Man, whose dominant values are expressed in terms of money, property, work for work's sake, science at the call of military powers and interests, technology bureaucratically applied, and all pursued to the point where we seem about to destroy our one real spaceship, the Earth itself.

MISS G:

Agreed! Agreed! But may we bring *you* back to our Earth again to tell us what, really, you want a teacher to be.

ME:

Right — and apologies for rocketing off. I'm for the teacher who tries to experience a poem, not exploit it in the interest of other teaching subjects. I want her or him to *hear* it just as I would want him to *feel* a wood carving. I want a teacher to be not merely the well-informed man — what Alfred North White-head called "the most useless bore on God's earth." I want him to be, in Whitehead's phrase, a person "with receptiveness to

67

beauty and humane feeling." I write a poem as an act of faith in the existence of humane and sensitive readers, whose imaginations are open to creativity and whose hearts love the infinite unpredictability and potentiality of all life. Perhaps I'm not wanting teachers to be teachers at all, but just good readers and listeners, devoted but discriminating; searching for what the eighteenth century oversimply called "the pleasures of the imagination"; above all, sharing and developing themselves as sharers of their pleasures with those younger beings who are the guests at their be-in. Creative readers become creative teachers.

MISS G:
I think you haven't quite landed yet. How about some examples of creative teaching and reading? How, for example, would you handle the mercy-killing element in your own poem?
(Bell rings) Oh dear, there's an assembly now!

ME:
Not to worry. I'll write the rest down and send it to you (and this is what I would have sent).

C. Creative Reading and Teaching

The Problem of Theme

I got a letter from a rural high school teacher in Saskatchewan which said: "Our class is taking your 'David.' Since the poet can always give the best interpretation of his poems, please send us yours...."

It is a fallacy that I can give the best interpretation of my poems because I wrote them. I can tell you what I thought I was up to when I wrote "David." But already I know I would say it a little differently if I were to try again this evening. And what I intended, and what I have done, are not the same things. What I have done is, in the long run, what others find in it. The poem, to live at all, will have to interpret itself after I'm dead. Moreover, each reviewer, critic, enthusiast or detractor whom I've ever heard on the subject of "David," interprets its aim, theme, and so on, at least slightly differently from every other. And this is right. This tells me the poem is at least challenging enough to trigger the different, the individual imaginations of each reader — provided the reader lets it. The poem is an invitation to explore, not a duty to explain.

What I treasure are the letters or critic's comments which say things about the poem I would have liked to. An example, for me, is a single sentence in Professor Robillard's recent study of my writings, in which he defines, far better than I could have, a major theme of "David": "When one's very *anima* — that which distinguishes one, and makes for the kind of life one lives — is wounded, physical death is preferable to spiritual death." (*op. cit.*, p. 15)

Morality (Euthanasia in "David")

I was fascinated by another letter, in 1955, from an Ontario girl whose grade 13 class had been asked to define "the basic problem in 'David'." They had come up with three: "the futility of mountain climbing, . . . the question of the advisability of euthanasia, . . . or mental conflict, man against his mind: Bobby's sense of right and wrong is in conflict with his desire to do David's wish." Okay, I suppose, as co-existing "subjects" but their teacher thought I should decide which was the real one, the one and only.

> *Ask me no questions, and I'll tell you no fibs.*
>
> *Oliver Goldsmith*

I wrote the student that all the solutions were right, and the teacher was wrong in presupposing there was one clearly major "problem," or indeed in thinking that the poem could be contained within three, or three thousand, moral concepts. I said:

. . . I don't write poems to make morals . . . I wrote 'David' to tell
a story, through which to communicate some of my complex feelings
about mountains and people . . . I don't think mountaineering any
more 'futile' than any other sport; one can make a case for any
human activity being futile, since we all die, whatever we do. Man
has been living for a million or more years, and not one person is
known by name or personality more than 10,000 years back. Most
have been forgotten within a generation. True, Bobby is plunged in
a conflict. But I don't decide if he does the "right thing." I decide
that Bobby *would* do what he did; i.e., that it is within human
capacity for a boy like Bob to have such sentiments and act that
way. *You* "judge," not me, whether the poem presents a possible life
experience and if it presents it in a way that has stirred your own
imagination and emotions. Don't demand more than that of a piece
of art. And tell me what conclusions your class came to.

I would have enjoyed knowing.

The act of euthanasia in the poem proved almost too controversial. In Ontario, for example, it seems a number of
Catholic teachers protested against having to teach a poem
that, in their words, "advocated mercy killing." Whether this
was a majority feeling among Ontario Catholic teachers is
something no one will ever know. Certainly many Ontario
nuns have spoken to me about the poem over the years, none
of whom disliked teaching it. Some noticed approvingly that
the mercy killer in "David" doesn't seem happy about his deed,
and, like the Ancient Mariner, is perhaps haunted by guilt and
compelled to retell his story in later years. They assured me
there was no actual church ban on my story; yet, the content
of the poem was enough to make some of them pause.

> *They that approve a private opinion, call it*
> *opinion; but they that mislike it, heresy.*
>
> **Thomas Hobbes**

Such attitudes, of course, concern me only in so far as they
operate to permit or prevent the circulation of my poem. I
don't share the religious dogma that a human being must be

70

prevented from ending his own life, whatever the circumstances, and never helped. For me, the circumstances in which I had placed Bobby can supply an argument to justify his act. He has, by his own awkwardness, caused an accident which has left his dearest friend dying, impaled on a remote ledge high on a Canadian mountain, with freezing night closing in. If David does not die quickly from his broken spine and other injuries, he will bleed to death or succumb to exposure before any rescue party can possibly reach him. Moreover David is paralyzed and cannot roll himself over the ledge and shorten the agonies of his death. He asks from Bobby only the benison that Bobby or any other human being would give a dying animal, the benison that David himself had given a crippled and doomed robin. In Bobby's position I think I'd have done what he did, and certainly in David's position I'd have asked for it.

"I kind of liked your poem," another student wrote to me, "but don't you think David would have been glad to be rescued, after he had thought it over in a wheelchair?" "Yes," I answered, "but not at the time, and the point is he hadn't a chance in hell of a wheelchair." In other words, I myself believe in euthanasia in certain situations and think that laws should be changed accordingly. I therefore regard this "theme" in my poem as a contemporary and controversial one for which I make no apologies.

Yet, having said all that, I don't believe this argument is of much relevance to the poem, or that the poem is propagandistic. If I had wanted to write an advocacy of mercy killing, I would have written a piece of prose with many examples and arguments, not a single incident, and I wouldn't have made my mercy killer a man haunted forever.

So, though I don't mind the teachers who assign essays on "Euthanasia, with specific reference to 'David'," I prefer the ones who ask their students whether David's request for it and Bobby's responses were consistent with their characters as portrayed in the poem. That approach can get understanding responses from students, such as these:

For David, death could be a kindness for he would not let anyone suffer.

The poem's climax made me for the first time *think* a lot about life and death.

Although I do not agree with Bob's decision, I think it was right for him and for David, and I think it would have taken a great deal of courage.[10]

If all moral problems found in poems were approached in a do-it-yourself spirit, with students projecting into the poem while retaining their own personalities, there would be no need for tests, essays, paraphrases, memorizations and examinations to ensure that a sufficient contact with literature had happened. Consideration of the poet's aim and determination of his personal moral position are useful only if they stimulate students to consider their own aims, ideas, concepts, ethics and aesthetics. Does the poet's "aim," once understood, provide *you* with an aim clearer or more satisfying? Or — much better, I think — have you, in the process, forgotten about morality, a concept for which the great Greeks had no word? Have you discovered the sheer enjoyment of the aesthetic experience and realized that it is also a progress in "knowing"? I don't really think poetry makes men "better," but it can make them temporarily both happier and more understanding of their fellows.

The "Meaning" of a Poem

This is a phrase used by persons who assume a poem has only one meaning, and they ought to know it. The meaning of "David" is what I put into it plus anything else you get out of it. In my poem, the meaning is almost always more than what is apparently there, and operates on various levels. It also varies according to the reader's basic language abilities and sensitivities, his acquaintance with other literature and with the background of the poem.

In any case, clarity, as I have said before, is only on the surface of a serious poem, and you will be all the more drawn

[10] For other reactions, see Appendix A.

into it because of that. No great art is ever enjoyed fully at first acquaintance. The language of poetry is complex, ambiguous, cunning and highly personal. It's not the language of your daily newspaper. It doesn't yield up single "right" answers to examination questions any more than life does. Perhaps the best way to get full meaning out of a poem is to forget about meaning when you read it. Instead, see with it, smell with it, touch with it, and above all hear with it. A poem is a total sensuous experience.

Hearing a Poem

I return to this subject because I think it's fundamental. Most of us begin to enjoy poetry earlier than we can remember, by listening to nursery rhymes. John Ciardi, the American poet in the preface to *Mid-Century American Poets,* remembers how the syllables of "Hickory Dickory Dock" were things he tasted on his tongue. And I remember it that way too, and as a spoon-beating ritual riddle, and a beautiful easy seeing of a quite impossible happening, climaxed when our own brindled Holstein jumped clear over the full Alberta moon. But I would have no such joy to recall if my mother had not *said* "Hickory Dickory Dock" to me and hummed it and swayed it with me.

"David" is meant to be a Hickory Dickory Dock too, as well as the text of an oratorio, and a possible movie, and a prompter for thinking about the values of life and death. Once it ceases to be all these things, it will pass into the limbo of dead verse, for it will no longer add to the reader's enjoyment of life. Most philosophers, be they Kierkegaard, Buddha, or Sartre, seem to agree in this: that satisfaction in life can exist only when three levels of living — feeling, thinking, acting — are continuing together. Even a poem must be able to operate this way. Certainly in the twenty years of my own experience in reading "David" to school children from grades 5 to senior matriculation and to university students at all levels, I have felt that the poem was alive only when there was an honest silence before any applause at the end of the reading, and spontaneous talking, criticizing and arguing about it afterwards with students, at least one of whom would finally make the gesture of showing me and reading me something he himself had written.

Creative Criticism

In many such encounters, as well as in letters sent me by students after class discussions, I can profit from their independent and imaginative criticisms. Sometimes it's just their meticulous attention to the muscular health of the poem, to a defect in credibility or in the realism, leaving me wishing I'd seen it myself in time to improve it. The ineptness of its title, the adjective too weak or too strong for its immediate task, the poverty of leads into character; nothing ultimately escapes the student eye.

Those forthright Antigonish students told their teacher that my two characters were "rather snobbish, looking down on their poker-playing, snoring companions on the survey." I suppose they were. I suppose I was when I was seventeen and lived a whole summer with five fixated card players in one small tent while a wilderness of great mountains lay all about, waiting to be explored. In my case, none of my companions would consent to climb on those golden weekends, but if I'd had a David I'm sure I'd have felt definitely superior to the poker fiends, much as I like poker. For them, what else was there to do but shuffle and sleep? We had no books or mail or telephone or radio — this was 1921 — and nothing but our own slash-trail out to other humans, a three-day slogging on foot. I think in this instance my psychology was right, but my poem has been outdated by technology. Survey camps are now likely to have two-way short waves, portable TV, and helicopters dropping *Time* (Canadian edition), mail and cartons of beer. I was writing of a generation most of whom are already dead.

Perhaps a less defensible detail, pointed out by another student, is Bobby's telling David (stanza 32) that he can "be back here by midnight with ropes." He knows this is a lie and knows that David knows. Why then would he say it? Well, if I were Bobby in that situation, I'd try all ways of making sure David would accept nothing but death, before taking over the dreadful responsibility for him. Students have argued, however, that Bobby wouldn't underrate David's intelligence by lying and would just wait dumbly till David's agony and insistence compelled him to comply. Perhaps. Depends on what kind of boy Bobby is.

An incident more than once questioned by classes is that in which David clings with one hand "to a dint in the scarp" while he uses his ice axe to get a grip above the overhang of a ridge. Then he "slipped from his hold and hung by the quivering pick,/Twisted his long legs up into space and kicked/To the crest." A girl in Oakville, Ontario wrote me "on behalf of the Fifth Form" that they "doubted the possibility of David, when hanging onto the pickaxe, being able to swing his legs up onto the ledge." It *is* possible, with an ice axe (see Appendix B) but not a pickaxe. This was a failure of communication between a climber and non-climbers, for this incident came from reality. A friend of mine and I, climbing without ropes, found a new route up Mount Girouard that way. We came up slantwise on a cliff face from the col of Inglismaldie, along ledges that petered out just under the safe southern slope leading to the peak. My companion was an experienced climber, nimble and cool, with strongly-developed arm muscles. The rock was firm, and we had no heavy clothing or equipment encumbering us. We got up in the way described, and I was happy to write the Oakville class a detailed reply, with a sketch. Their close attention to text cheered me and, I hope, their teacher, undoubtedly the one who had fostered it. I was happier still to get a reply to the effect that I'd convinced them.

The most original twist to the poem ever proposed to me was made only recently by a teacher who evidently had been brooding about the character of Bobby, off and on, since she'd taken the poem in a grade 10 British Columbia class. "I believe," she wrote me, "that David's companion was a female . . . Did you write this poem with the thought in mind . . . ? I have discussed this with many different people . . . but very few, if any, agree with me." The reasons she offered were somewhat vague, largely that "Bob's relationship with David is . . . a dependent and hero-worshipping (as well as loving) one." How should one answer? I wrote that though it wasn't my intention to make Bobby a female, I certainly intended him to be dependent, hero-worshipping and loving in relation to David. From there on, the characterization in the poem is a free thing with a life of its own. Anyone's at liberty to find what he wants in it for himself. On the psychological level, Bobby is perhaps unconsciously or half-consciously homosexual in his feeling for David — or he's "feminine," if you prefer. On the realistic narrative level, he would have needed to be a fantastically successful transvestite to remain undetected in a wilderness survey camp. In my day, at least, women were not hired for such jobs. But I'm happy to feel the poem has yet another dimension, for one reader at least, and a dimension that just might help it survive the Women's Revolution.

Responsive Creation

That last example is not so much one of creative criticism as of an independent creation offered in response to mine. This can become the most heart-warming of all reader reactions for the poet. The alternative creations triggered can take many forms, ranging from a sensitive speaking of the poem by such a gifted professional actor as René Auberjonois, or the comic high school parody of Tom Franck's that I've already mentioned, to something more spontaneous and powerful, a response of action. I once received a letter from a girl who had been brought up in a big Eastern city, telling me that after she had read my poem as an undergraduate eight years earlier, she had sought out a summer job as a waitress in Banff in order to see mountains at last, "to look for valleys the moon could be rolled in." She found climbing both exhausting and terrifying "but the loneliness was the most exhilarating thing I've ever experienced. Now I return to the Rockies whenever I can," she wrote me from an advertising writer's desk in Detroit, "because they are beautiful and cold and uncompromising, and some day I will find a secret there . . ."

This sort of re-creation in action is typical of the young of today, and it's exciting. As Marshall McLuhan has put it, they're concerned not "with the educational process but the package." They're not content with information about Dar-es-Salaam or Mysore; instead they join CEDA and get a job, and they go there.

But I value equally those immediate responses within the classroom that lead to more literary creativity, like that of a teacher and her grade 11 pupils in Toronto some years ago. She asked them simply "to write *anything* expressing thoughts about the poem." They did and the results were read aloud. The next step was the formation of a spontaneous committee from the class to select the best pieces of their own writing and shoot them across Canada to me. Among them there was even a definition of poetry:

> Poetry is the something
> that makes one stretch his mind
> and wander . . .
> to seek the Meaning.

I'm not claiming that this is itself poetry, but I think it reflects the mind of a teacher who understood poetry. There could be much more of this, more schools like the Toronto one which began an experiment in the language arts that resulted in the production of sixty works of fiction, typed, bound and illustrated by the students themselves. The ages of these pupils at Huron Street Public School in Toronto ranged between eight and twelve.

Creativity is a common human power and its expression is a human right. Any teacher of the arts who doesn't succeed in stimulating more creativity is a handicap to the child and to his growth into a healthy, loving adult. Stimulating isn't all that hard. Any good writing, whether in prose or poetry, sets off a desire to hear it pronounced, because the excellence lies in the use of words, and words are not only idea-symbols on a page, they are sounds. The point of departure from dull classroom routine into the world of the pleasures of the imagination happens when a teacher or student is moved to exclaim, "That's good, let's hear it!" And then it is sounded, not because it's a fine example for all of the violation of rule 92a regarding dangling gerundives (or is it gerunds?), but because it makes a special literary music, something that has grown out of the ancient heritage of incantation and yet carries the true voice of the child who wrote it.

Nor is it merely the so-called gifted child who can be thus encouraged. "Any child can be attuned to poetry by any good teacher" says the American poet, Kenneth Koch.[11] He knows; he recently edited a whole book of poems written in an "underprivileged" Manhattan school. Of all the arts, I think that of writing is the most natural and the most rewarding to encounter in the classroom. Its technique comes largely from common instinct and the unconscious learning process at the beginning of acquiring language. It's natural to practise writing, as it's not, except for the gifted few, to practise on the piano. Creative writing is exactly the activity which can loosen the uptight school atmosphere, let children go at their own pace, and provide that informality which, in the words of Charles E. Silberman:

> relieves the teacher of the terrible burden of omniscience. In a traditional classroom it is difficult — and threatening — for any but the most secure teacher to admit ignorance . . . In an informal classroom . . . the teacher is the facilitator rather than the source of learning, the source being the child himself. Learning is something the child makes happen to and for himself, albeit with the teacher's aid and sometimes at her instigation. The consequence is an atmosphere in which everyone is learning together.[12]

And is what's learned "useful"? Surely it offers the usefulness that all creativity gives, of exercising the critical faculties, including the self-critical; of developing one's sensitivity to the pleasures of communication; of providing a therapy, a voice to assert, endure and overcome the frustrations of the spirit that assail us all; it is, moreover, a stimulus to emotional honesty, a way of preserving and honouring the child still within us. It is also one of the few ways of hope left us in a society becoming

11 "Ah Poets," *Time* (December 28, 1970), p. 26. Also see Kenneth Koch, *Wishes, Lies and Dreams* (New York: Random House, 1971).
12 Charles Silberman, "Murder in the Classroom, Part I," *Atlantic Monthly* (July 1970), p. 86.

increasingly conformist and self-despairing, violent, meaning-less and death-bent. Such a society is by its very nature inimical to free creativity, for creativity is a power that grows out of peace and joy. There are perhaps only two such powers, when all is said. One is love and the other is art. Love rests on the preservation of our species; art is our instinctive instrument for the preservation of the individual, of the unique man, woman and child, and the means of evolution of us all into something able and worthy of survival on the living earth.

3 WRITING AND READING:
SOME LYRICS AND SATIRICS

I don't take your words
merely as words.
Far from it.

I listen
to what makes you talk—
Whatever that is—
And me listen.

Shinkichi Takahashi

Nearly everything I've said so far has had some relation to "David," a somewhat impersonal story-poem, despite its first-person narrator. The writing of lyrical and of satirical poetry are naturally somewhat different acts and lead, in consequence to different approaches in reading. In this chapter I'll be talking about ten of my own poems, chosen because they are among those easily available to students in *Five Modern Canadian Poets*[1] and because I think they represent some of my best short poems in the twenty years following "David," that is, 1942-62. Since, like most poets, I kept moving or changing in techniques and attitudes, it may be of some help to students if I discuss these poems in their time-order.

[1] ed. Eli Mandel (Toronto: Holt, Rinehart & Winston, 1970), pp. 7-22; in addition this anthology contains "Bear on the Delhi Road" which I will not discuss here, since I've already talked at some length about it in *The Creative Writer*, pp. 16-17.
A list of available texts for each of these poems is provided at the end of this chapter.

Vancouver Lights

Professor Bentley asks (Mandel, *op. cit.*, p. 22): "Is this a description of the lights of Vancouver . . . or something else?" The answer, I think, is, as with most literary questions, "both." This poem unfortunately is not deathless, and must be understood in relation to the time of its writing.

The second stanza describes the blackouts spreading from Europe through North Africa, over to Halifax, and now threatening the lights of Vancouver. That should date it as 1941. But isn't there a reference in the last stanza to the atom bomb, which no one, except the Allied top brass, knew about until one was dropped on Hiroshima in 1945?

The truth is that the poem began in my head as early as 1923, when I was an undergraduate of nineteen. In those days I used to join climbing parties into the mountains north of Vancouver. After the last Friday class we would dispose of the first three thousand feet by walking up a trail to Grouse Plateau, before moving on to the real climbing on the Camel or the Lions the next day. From the Plateau, before the pollution, the city's lights were spread out like another range of the heavens. One such night, images and phrases crowded into my thoughts as I sat.

Back in town I began a descriptive poem, in a mood of simple delight and awe in the beauty of things. I worked to make it the best poem I could, but I was afraid to show it to anyone, fearful of further rebuffs such as I'd already had from professors and fellow-students. I'd saved enough to buy my first typewriter, a very old machine with a worn ribbon and chipped keys. I typed up the poem, wrote a letter of submission (my very first), enclosed a stamped return envelope as I'd heard one must, and addressed everything to the only place I could think of that might publish it, the Vancouver *Province*. (There were no literary journals at all, west of Toronto, in those years.) But I kept losing my nerve at the mailbox and putting the letter back in my pocket. Twice I pried up the flap, made inky revisions and resealed the envelope. At least a month passed before I got enough courage to bang the lot into the slot, and another three before the reaction came.

"Dear Sir," it read, "If you have no better opinion of your poem than to send me such a misbegotten and slovenly copy of it as I now return, how can you expect . . ." etc. The literary editor went on to say he liked the poem little better than my typing; he gave no suggestions as to how I might improve either. I put my misbegotten one away in a growing heap of aborted masterpieces.

It was indeed 1941, eighteen years later in Toronto, when I dug it out again, in the middle of that mood of nostalgia for mountains which led to the writing of "David." Now it was easy for me to see how little I'd said at nineteen, and how wordily I'd said it. But the visual details were still alive enough to send me back in my imagination to that same ridge to look again at Vancouver's lights.— this time with the knowledge that they might, any moment now, be blacked or even bombed out, with the houses themselves, by the annihilation that was spreading ever westward. Halifax lay in self-imposed darkness while raiding submarines cruised under the Bay of Fundy. Would all the world's lamps be doused? And who would re-light them? It eased my own gloom to turn those old notes into a sort of letter-poem to the future, in hope there would still be someone in it who could, and would, read me.

As for the apparent reference to atom bombs, it was simply a lucky turn of phrase. In 1941, what are now called "conventional weapons" seemed terrible and powerful enough to snuff us all out. The poem's topicality made it easy to get it printed. After one or two rejections it found a place in the first number of a new Toronto journal, long dead now.

Any student interested in poets' revisions might find some morbid interest in that first version, for it contained a whole stanza suppressed in all later ones.[2] I've often wished I'd cut it even more. For me, the poem belongs to an early "rhetorical" period of my writing; it's too adjectival, over-elaborate with

---

2 See *Canadian Review of Music and Art*, I, 5 (June 1942), 8; a copy is in the Birney Collection, Rare Books and Manuscript Section, University of Toronto Library.

sound-echoings, tautologies, half-rhymes and formal, even archaic phrasings. I was trying to get a "troubled delight" by a slow pace and compact phrasing, but I overdid it. The five-stress assonantal couplets would in themselves have given the rhythm sufficient weight and *andante* for the mood of reverie. It's true that "Vancouver Lights" has since made over a score of appearances and continues to be anthologized, but I suspect this is less because of the way it's written than because what it says has remained all too "contemporary."

It's over-late to alter, though I've lately risked six small revisions,[3] and eliminated all punctuation except two question marks and a dash, replacing the original little forest of squiggles with white spaces. Professor Bentley asks, "How does this affect one's interpretation of the poem?" My hope is that the comma-purge has reduced the sense of rhetorical heaviness. But students should make their own decision about that, as well as about everything else they read or hear.

Mappemounde

> *Et je suis de nouveau reporté sur la mer indif-*
> *férente et liquide. Quand je serai mort, on ne*
> *me fera plus souffrir.*
> **Paul Claudel**

"Mappemounde" is the sort of thing that can trigger complaints about obscurity and endless arguments about "meaning." I won't repeat what I've said about the pleasures of complexity, symbolism, even criticism in a poem. On the other hand, I won't defend this poem simply because it is complex. Instead, I want to suggest a simple way of leading into it, and perhaps into other seemingly difficult poems. The way is through the title.

---

[3] These changes are in lines 3, 5, 10, 21, 22, 38 of the version in Mandel. If I were preparing a further revision I would delete the following words: *sable, Streaming, lambent, cunningly, rulered with manplot the velvet chaos.* They seem to me to add nothing.

In Canada, most poetry readers have at least a little high school French; with that, or with a dictionary as elementary as my *Vest Pocket French-English*, a student will discover that the word means "map of the world." The apparent misspelling (*-mounde* for *-monde*) is simply the medieval one. This is the thread into the poem's little maze of early notions of the Earth: a single continent surrounded by one dreadful ocean. My images are prompted by those strange designs which scribes placed in the corners of that perilous sea, the "mere that squares our map." Its outer boundaries were the edges of the flat Earth, over which the too adventurous ships tumbled, sinking through whirlpool (*maelstrom*) to hell itself. Even if a sailor escaped that fate, he might succumb to the sea serpents (*nadders*, the Saxons called them — an older form of *adder*) or to the treacherous mermaids, those sirens whose songs made the sailor-heroes of Ulysses forget in an instant their sweethearts back in the very homes they were bound for. There were mermen too (why not?), swimming up to shore to cast lovespells on unwary ladies. And, of course, that whale Cetegrande, the great Cetacean long as an island who swallowed ships whole.

The poem can now be seen to be made up really of one image, supplied in the title and elaborated to the end. But many individual words can still give trouble unless the student lets himself slide not only into medieval images but into medieval language habits and rhythms, especially those developed by the first English poets, the writers of *Beowulf* and *The Seafarer*. For "Mappemounde," even though it has the line-count of a Renaissance sonnet, is much earlier in its form. Each line is divided into halves and, in most cases, the first half makes single or double alliterations with the second (e.g., A*d*read in that *m*ere we *d*rift to *m*ap's end). Moreover the rhythms are not "regular" in the way of post-medieval poetry; they can't be scanned into iambics and all that; they are the Old English speech rhythms based on three kinds of natural accents: a heavy primary, a lighter but still definite secondary, and an unaccented syllable. This is really the normal accent pattern of our speech today, despite all the attempts of pedants to make us hear ourselves in pseudo-Greek cadences. So the first half-line reads "NO *not* this OLD" — or BÓOM bòm dĕ BÓOM, and the second half: BÓOM bòm dĕ BÓOM dĕ.

One must take into account medieval language habits too. Old English scops (poets) delighted in what they called "kennings" or figurative substitutes for the ordinary word. To call the sea merely the sea was to admit your inability as a poet. So it became the swanroad, the gull's bath, or the whalehall, as in my poem where, by the same principle, the memory of loved ones becomes the breast-hoard, and so on.

Is the poem still obscure? Perhaps, but I'd hope that what's left is the right kind of obscurity, the multiple ambiguity that interpenetrates most poems if they're effective at all, the thing that makes the reader's imagination take off on its own flight, without caring if he's caught exactly all the nuances the author intended.

> *Let such teach others who themselves excel,*
> *And censure freely who have written well.*
>
> *Alexander Pope*

But certainly this is the sort of poem which justifies editorial notes for a student not yet advanced in his knowledge of earlier literature and language. Is this a defect? Again, each reader must decide individually.

In case it might be of help, I'll try to put down what I was hoping to make happen. Think of the speaker as a man, ancient or modern, saying goodbye to his girl before setting out across an ocean or some other bigness of space. But really, he's more concerned with the map of time for it's the years, not the miles, that make lovers forget. Time's the enemy of us all, the beast that catches up with any world that's willing to set aside loving for voyages into seas of hate.

However, the poem is intended not as moral allegory so much as Hardyean irony. I began it in 1945 in England while I lay in a crowded military sickbay, waiting for a hospital ship to take me home, listening meantime to the exchanges of eternal fidelity between nearby wardmates and their English girl friends. Our ship, the *El Nil* (ironically, once the private yacht of that old roué, King Farouk), brought us safely to Halifax, but it was my impression that many of those English girls would be detained by mermen on their Anglosaxon shores and many of our seafarers lose their pledges to Cetegrande before map's end.

Here are two opposite opinions of the poem for students to consider:

Frank Davey: one of Birney's questionably successful attempts to bring Anglo-Saxon stoicism to the hardships of World War II.

(*Earle Birney*, p. 82)

Al Purdy: I am not a critic but a poet, and do not hold "Mappe-mounde" beside other great poems. This is not necessary. It stands alone, without company, beautiful — odd, old-Saxon jargon that is queerly imminent as death. It brings all the old maps and youthful stories of explorers floating back on your tide . . .

(letter, 1955)

From the Hazel Bough

Le sein charmant qui joue avec le feu,
Le sang qui brille aux lèvres qui se rendent
Les derniers dons, les doigts qui les défendent,
Tout va sous terre et rentre dans le jeu!

Paul Valéry

I wrote all but the final stanza of this poem in my head one night, while I was still in military hospital in Toronto. The nub of what I have to say about "From the Hazel Bough" is available in John R. Colombo's *How Do I Love Thee,* a collection of poets' own favourites with their reasons for choices.

It's also the favourite among all my shorter poems with editors, composers and critics, having appeared in a good number of journals and anthologies in half a dozen countries. Nevertheless it had to struggle into print. The poem was rejected in Canada, and first saw daylight in an obscure quarterly, the *University of Kansas City Review,* from where it travelled to the "Poet's Column" of the *New York Times Book Review.* An American editor, seeing it there, included the poem in an "American Poets Number" he was guest-editing for a New Zealand magazine. From New Zealand, it was submitted to an international committee selecting the best English language poems appearing anywhere that year. They gave the poem first prize and sent a cheque to the unknown New Zealander, whereupon I established my identity and was at last able to get the poem accepted in Canada. What's meant by calling a poet "Canadian"?

Although the basic rhythm was suggested to me quite irrelevantly by "Casey Jones," it's been possible for composers to set it to their own sort of music, each wildly different: stark neoclassical from Montreal's Alexander Brott; jazz from Toronto's Calvin Winters; far-out atonal from the American Warren Benson. But some have found the poem of no interest; the author of a recent 128-page study of my work fails even to mention "From the Hazel Bough."

Canada: Case History

Be wise, and ne'er to publick view produce
Thy undrest Mistress, or unfinisht Muse...

William Wycherley

I've never thought of this as a poem. It's a piece of satire in verse: that is, sharp, rational remarks set out in the lines of traditional poetry, and carrying alternate rhyme to point up the attempts at wit, but in both viewpoint and language essentially topical. This kind of writing can have an immediate popular success and in a few years become so out-of-date in both phrasing and message that it's lost all value except to literary or social historians. I think "Canada: Case History" has had a longer run than it merits. Since its publication in 1947 (after six rejections by other Canadian magazines), it has been reprinted thirty-three times, including translations into Italian and Hungarian! I suppose it caught on because anthologists liked to have some pithy verses summing up "Canada Today," and there weren't many alternates to choose from. Yet its first editor, B. K. Sandwell of *Saturday Night*, accepted it under the assumption that it was simply a character study of some teenager, for he wrote me, proposing to correct the "typographical error" of "land" to "lad" in the first line!

Why was I prompted to manufacture this squib? Well,

World War Two had involved me in making psychological case reports on literally thousands of Canadian soldiers. When I came back, I started looking at the rest of my fellow-Canadians at home from the viewpoint of an interpreter of my country to other nations; I was now supervising Radio Canada's foreign-language broadcasts to Europe, and making weekly visits to External Affairs in Ottawa to keep acquainted with relevant Canadian foreign policies. I decided that, for the year 1946 at least, I knew enough about the Canadian character to write a casual portrait of it in the jargon of a caseworker's report on a "problem adolescent." My motivation was thus intellectual, not poetic. I was interested only in needling my compatriots into realizing that we hadn't yet produced an adult national identity.

Within a few years I felt the piece was quite inadequate to describe the changes in Canadianism, and the continuing demand for it by teachers compiling textbooks made me gloomily aware that there were a lot of teachers as out-of-date as my case history. When the Confederation Centennial caught up with us, I couldn't stand it any longer, and composed a new report about "an undergraduate land . . . sexually no longer stealthy," only "almost good at sports" and "so-so healthy," no longer slow "at turning down dares"; becoming narcissistic, I added: ". . . Most of the estate already mortgaged south./ Prognosis? In the Centennial Year I should shut my big mouth."

It proved easy to shut. Nobody would print the thing, and anyway by 1969 I had a still later version, which *Saturday Night* published, and which I included in a paperback selection of my poems in that year (*Poems of Earle Birney*, p. 9). But this third case history had barely begun to circulate when its predictions of French-English disunity were over-confirmed by the Quebec crisis of 1970, and I had to write a fourth version in 1971. I include that one here, for student interest. I've had no success in publishing it, except in a so-called underground nationalist paper in Vancouver, which took it, perhaps, largely for political reasons.

canada: case history: 1971

No more the highschool land
deadset in loutishness
this cat's turned cool and cruel
the gangling's gone
guffaws are for the peasants

Inside his plastic igloo now he watches
gooks & yankees bleed in color on the telly
but underneath his Carnaby shirt the knives
of pain are flashing thru an ulcerous belly

Hung up on rye and nicotine and sex-
y mags, kept off the snow and grass
he teeters tiptoe on his arctic roof
(ten brittle legs no two together)
baring his royal canadian ass
white and helpless in the global winds

Schizoid for sure and now a sado-masochist
this turkey thinks that for his sins
he ought to be served up while still alive:
legs to Quebec (a future Vietnam?)
the rest self-carved and pre-digested
to make a Harvest Home for Uncle Sam . . .

Teeth shot and memory going
(except for childhood grudges)
one moment murderous the next depressed
this youth we fear has moved from adolescence
into what looks like permanent senescence.

Query: What word-uses, images, attitudes are already stale in this version?

So now I ask you, my student readers: if you wanted to present a versified satire of Canada in nineteen-whatever-it-is, would you use any one of these versions, and if so which, and why? As for myself, I've withdrawn permission for further printing of any of them. I'm tired of being forced, by this jeremiad, to pose as a permanent sociological judge-and-jury of my own country, in the name of poetry. Poetry is something else. Right?

Ellesmereland I and II

To see a World in a Grain of Sand,
And a Heaven in a Wild Flower.

William Blake

Ellesmereland I

Explorers say that harebells rise
from the cracks of Ellesmereland
and cod swim fat beneath the ice
that grinds its meagre sands
No man is settled on that coast
The harebells are alone
Nor is there talk of making man
from ice cod bell or stone

1952

Ellesmereland II

And now in Ellesmereland there sits
a town of twenty men
They guard the floes that reach to the Pole
a hundred leagues and ten
The warders watch the sky watch them
the stricken hills eye both
A mountie visits twice a year
And there is talk of growth

1965

All poetry, all art, is somewhat topical, of course. Verbal art, anyway. Languages are living things that eventually grow old and fade away. Nobody understands Etruscan. Even poems expressing apparent "eternals" can suffer in a few months or years from a small turn of events. "Ellesmereland" was composed in 1952, after I'd read an explorer's account of a visit to that island whose farthest tip is the most northern land on earth. It was said to be uninhabited by man; there was a brief summer when blue harebells bloomed. My small poem about it appeared the next year in *The Canadian Forum,* but by that time a missile-tracking station had been set up on Ellesmere, and the poem's immediate pertinence was lost. Nobody seems to have noticed the verse until six years later, when it reappeared in the *Atlantic Monthly.* For the Canadian writer, nothing succeeds at home like publication abroad. In no time "Ellesmereland" had been reprinted in a Secondary School Teachers' Bulletin, and then duly analysed and expounded to students; reprinted again in England; translated into Spanish; published in Ecuador; read over CBC and BBC and enshrined and footnoted in a succession of school texts.

It's called "Ellesmereland I" because in 1965 I wrote a companion piece, "Ellesmereland II," to report on the military occupation. But the first poem has proved to be better, though those who like it disagree rather widely about what they think it means. For example, the Dean of the Ontario College of Education suggested, in 1960, one way in which the poem "may have come into existence":

> Hardly has man won freedom from his subservience to nature than he becomes a victim of the will of his fellow man. There are people and nations that would make man a captive creature, brainwash his mind and make him over to suit their needs. The next step would be the making of a whole man, a living robot. Speculating on this idea a poet turns back to nature to see how the creatures thrive. In the process of this preparation to think, this incubating of an idea, this illuminating of a pattern and this verification of an idea in the form of a finished poem, the poet may well have seen red and then cooled off to a startling contrast in black and white. Once his hand set to work, he shaped a spearhead with a razor's edge. [4]

[4] B. C. Diltz, "The Creative Imagination and the Educational System," *Bulletin of the Ontario Secondary School Teachers Assoc.,* XL, 2 (March 31, 1960), 77.

Another educationalist, Harold Dew, wrote me, disagreeing with this interpretation. For him "the poem's central meaning [lay] in the startling contrast between harmonious nature in a very bleak place and man as a rather sorry experiment, an intruder on nature." (5 May, 1960)

Here is part of my reply:

> . . . What the poem conveys to others, only others know . . . The Arctic far-north struck me as a symbol of Survival — an elemental complex of living forms which might even last through the destruction by man of the living world, including himself . . . But if evolution had to start over again from some place like Ellesmereland it might never get beyond fish and flower; the laws of chance would dictate otherwise; and certainly if there was anything *sentient* about evolution, there would be a decision *not* to proceed toward man again, the creature who brought the holocaust. Man would simply not be talked of.

I'd put it slightly differently today. After all, the poem was written in the course of an hour or so, over twenty years ago. I must interpret it now, less from the memory of writing it than from what it says to me, just another reader, in 1972.

El Greco: Espolio

In 1953 I saw a retrospective El Greco exhibition in Bordeaux. One painting that both captured and puzzled me was his *Espolio*, an imagining of the scene when Christ waited on the Hill of Calvary before his execution. Meantime he endured the Espolio or "spoliation" (Latin *expolio*, that is, "despoiling"), a tearing away of his clothes by greedy spectators who would then gamble for the strips.[5] In his painting, there is a prominent figure in the right foreground, in workmen's clothes, whom I take to be the carpenter; he is busy putting holes in the cross.

---

[5] If what I've just said isn't clear to the student, this is a good time for him to look up *Matthew* 27:35, or *Mark* 15:24, or *Luke* 23:34-35, or best of all, *John* 19:23-24, and become perhaps more confused. In El Greco's painting, the garments are being taken off, as one might expect, *before* the actual crucifying; in all four gospels, it seems they crucify him first.

Seven years after I saw the original in Bordeaux, a publisher sent me a cropped reproduction of the "Espolio," which focussed attention on the lower half of the painting, and so on the carpenter. I realized that someone else must surely have been caught by the strangeness of making the most immediate figure in the painting not Christ but his executioner. I now noticed also that the eyes of the Virgin and the other women were fixed on this same subsidiary figure, whose back was actually turned to Christ. What was El Greco driving at?

We'll never know for sure but we can all make guesses. I took the publisher's ad away with me that weekend to a friend's place on Bowen Island, my writing retreat in those years. And my own guess began to verbalize inside me. But the poem that resulted wasn't really a guess; I was far too unskilled as an interpreter of visual art to come forward with any "thesis" about El Greco's canvas. All I could try to do was to unravel the thoughts it had set going in my head, to think about craftsmanship, one of the elements in art that links its creator with carpenters, engineers, farmers, housewives, with everybody who employs a skill to earn a living. There's a curious peace that comes in the intensity of practising one's métier, an absorption that annihilates time and place.

El Greco: Espolio

The carpenter is intent on the pressure of his hand

on the awl and the trick of pinpointing his strength
through the awl to the wood   which is tough
He has no effort to spare for despoilings
or to worry if he'll be cut in on the dice
His skill is vital to the scene   and the safety of the state
Anyone can perform the indignities   It's his hard arms
and craft that hold the eyes of the convict's women
There is the problem of getting the holes exact
(in the middle of this elbowing crowd)
and deep enough to hold the spikes
after they've sunk through those bared feet
and inadequate wrists he knows are waiting behind him

He doesn't sense perhaps that one of the hands
is held in a curious gesture over him —
giving or asking forgiveness? —
but he'd scarcely take time to be puzzled by poses
Criminals come in all sorts   as anyone knows who makes crosses
are as mad or sane as those who decide on their killings
Our one at least has been quiet so far
though they say he talked himself into this trouble
a carpenter's son who got notions of preaching

Well heres a carpenter's son who'll have carpenter sons
God willing   and build what's wanted   temples or tables
mangers or crosses   and shape them decently
working alone in that firm and profound abstraction
which blots out the bawling of rag-snatchers
To construct with hands   knee-weight   braced thigh
keeps the back turned from death

But it's too late now for the other carpenter's boy
to return to this peace before the nails are hammered

Bowen Island 1960

Professor Bentley has asked readers, "What would be lost if the title were omitted . . . ?" (Mandel, *op. cit.*, p. 22) I've been suggesting that a great deal of what I intended might be lost. It's true that the now-privileged minority who have some knowledge of the Bible might find an "in" pleasure by gradually becoming aware, without help from a title, that this poem is about the Crucifixion. But the poem springs from contemplating a great painter's work, and I want to acknowledge and establish that indebtedness before my words begin, if only that those who also know the painting may be alerted.

What happens when even part of the title is dropped may be seen in the National Film Board's current cinematic treatment of the poem, called simply *Espolio*. The word is not explained or translated and El Greco is not mentioned, nor is the painting ever shown as a whole on the screen. This deliberate (and unauthorized) mystification leaves the viewer clueless as to the poem's intention, and considerably bored.

Another aspect of the poem not transmitted in the film and yet, to my mind, integral is what Professor Mandel calls "the laconic voice of the speaker," which he suggests "reinforces the extraordinary intensity of the scene of torment that gives focus to the action." (Mandel, *op. cit.*, p. 7) However, I'm not at all sure that I've handled this "voice" consistently in the poem itself. Perhaps it wavers between El Greco's and the carpenter's, or between an ironic observer of the Crucifixion and a sympathetic interpreter of the painting itself. Each reader ought to decide whether this uncertainty of voice is engaging or merely confusing. An interesting point for technical comparison is Auden's masterly use of "voice" in his poem about another painting, Brueghel's *Icarus*. Has the "speaker" a consistent personality there?

I suggest that anyone interested in further discussion of this poem should read the detailed analysis of it made by Professor Richard Robillard in his recent study of my work.

A Walk in Kyoto

Written in 1958, shortly after a brief lecture-visit to Japan, this is a traveller's poem. On one level, I feel it to be a record of a day's half-conscious hunting for a bridge of identity between my raw Canadian self and the subtle complexities of Japan's ancient capital, Kyoto. I'm searching for certain common human principles of hope, strength, vigour, natural joy; I find them in a small boy, one of tens of thousands who on this annual Boys' Day are flying special kites made in the likeness of a golden carp, a Japanese virility symbol.

I think the poem runs clearly enough without further comment from me, though perhaps it helps to know beforehand who Gulliver is; that I'm nine inches taller than the average Japanese; that in the classical drama *(kabuki)* men play all the women's roles; that in the modern "Ladies' Opera" *(takarazuka)* women play all the men's roles; that written Japanese is made up of Chinese characters, plus two separate Japanese scripts to signify the grammar; that shoguns were feudal lords, and their surviving castles, turned to museums, are often labelled Important Cultural Property, under a law designed to protect art objects from vandalism; that Zen is a variety of Buddhism, some of whose concepts may be symbolized in flower arrangements; and that in Kyoto there is a five hundred-ton statue of Buddha.

All this doesn't hurt, but it doesn't help much either. You won't turn on to this "Walk" by asking for information about Kyoto. You'll find it by interrelating your walk with mine. I feel that's what the following two readers have done:

> *Eli Mandel:* The contrast between the giant Westerner and the Lilliputian Orientals, particularly the startling reversal which, following on a confrontation with the Lord Buddha, suddenly shrinks the poet himself into a Lilliputian [shows] the contemporary writer exploit[ing] his oddly-tilted world for comic effect as well as thematic development.
>
> (*Five Modern Canadian Poets*, p. 3)

> *Richard Robillard:* The closing scene picks up [earlier] images and transforms them into symbols of heroic freedom. The maid's . . . delight in the boy is figured in the opening of the flower to the sun . . . [and] the whole quest for male vigor in a conventionalized society ends in the simple artifice of a boy's kite.
>
> (*Earle Birney*, p. 76)

Six-Sided Square: Actopan

In 1955 I went to Mexico for the first time and stayed for a long summer. Leonard Brooks, the painter, took me on some of his sketching trips into half-medieval mountain towns and wild jungle villages off the tourist routes. When I came back to Canada I encountered a practical dowager who had never been south of the Rio Grande and was puzzled as to why the people weren't more comprehensible, more, say, like Ontarians. I found myself tongue-tied by her simplistic questions, and I let off my frustration later in a tumbling *jeu d'esprit*, a what-I-should-have-said.

The poem as printed in Mandel is incomplete. It should be encased by six slightly interrupted lines, forming the actual shape and  entrances of Actopan's curious hexagonal plaza, (as in my *Selected Poems*). A trivial complaint, made only because the omission does blur my concept, which includes the *visual* strangeness.

Sinaloa

I know the tunes
of every bird,
but I found these words and song
in the tongue
of the strident partridge

Alkman

The following summer I returned to Mexico, this time driving down the west coast. In the second state south of the border, Sinaloa, I came through huge federal irrigation projects designed to turn the stretching deserts into an infinitely expanding supply of export-quality fruits and vegetables for the U.S. market. I talked to some of the new Mexicans this economy was evolving, men who had no desire to ride burros or sit under sombreros watching sunsets and making pots for tourists. Now, while rich American sportsmen were still hunting vanishing jaguars in the jungles, these Sinaloans were hunting money in the mushrooming city ports, trading in thousand-ton-lots of sugar and cotton, and boasting of profits over cocktails in air-conditioned motels. Later I listened to a tipsy machinery salesman in a cantina in Guanajuato, a man with a magnificent flow of Latinamerican English. He too had "bought" the whole Progress Package, and cared as little for ecology and the future as he did for tourists and the past. He both exhilarated and horrified me; I tried to suggest this contradiction through letting him talk in my poem. I thought the irony showed, in a fun way at least. But there's been at least one professor of English, unable to distinguish the "voice" of a poem from that of the poet himself, who has recently classified this poem as a satire of "the *lack* of industrialization in Central America"![6] As Chaucer would say, those were the rooster's words, not mine.

For George Lamming

Since few North Americans read West Indian literature, I attached a note to this poem when it first appeared in Canada which mentioned that George Lamming had written an autobiography of his early years in Barbados called *In the Castle of My Skin*. I might have added that he is also a leading novelist, poet and lecturer, but my memo was designed only to clarify the poem's opening and acknowledge my indebtedness to Lamming for its final image.

The poem as a whole is an admission of a greater indebtedness to George Lamming who, without any previous knowledge of me, committed himself to being my chief host, guide and chairman during a week in 1962 when I came to Kingston, Jamaica, to read and lecture on Canadian poetry. I had so much to thank him for formally, and such warm personal affection for him too, that when I got on board my ship to Trinidad and sat down to write him a letter, this poem came out instead. For as so often with me when my memory goes back over a complex experience, one moment of heightened sensation will outshine everything else. Not a predictable moment, either — something almost irrelevant, trivial, even silly — but loaded with symbolism for me. The poem relives such a moment and conveys, for most readers whose reactions I know about, something of the explosion of meaning/feeling which happened within me.

[6] Frank Davey, *Earle Birney* (Toronto: Copp Clark, 1972), p. 81; my emphasis.

Not for all. One critic has found the poem only another example of my vain "romantic hope for social harmony" and my "loss of grip on language" that leads me "quickly into sentimentality."[7] A possible reply is that the poem is not expressing a *hope* for social harmony but reporting an *occurrence* of it. As for such words as "romantic" and "sentimental," they become, when they're used without a hint of definition, only faded clichés betraying the green critic. There's always a danger of soppiness, of course, in writing down feelings of pleasure, gratitude, love, but poets must take such a risk, and to hell with the pedants.

> *Writing is a sweet and wonderful reward, but for what?...I am sitting here in the comfortable position of a writer, ready to accept all things beautiful, and must watch idly when my real Ego, poor and defenseless,... is being pinched, thrashed, and almost ground to dust by the devil.*
>
> *Franz Kafka*

It's the objects of his affection he should care about; will *they* be embarrassed, or misunderstand? There's a challenge there, and a greater one if the emotion to be conveyed is tied up with irrational but quite real and natural feelings of "white" guilt, suddenly felt in the presence of black friendship. That's why the poem begins: "To you I can risk . . ." One trusts a fellow-poet to hear the resonance behind the word, intuit the nuances of feeling, and so forgive the clumsiness of speaking at all on such a subject.

The word "guilt" is itself inadequate, of course, and I avoid it in the poem. You must move about in a country of black people whose ancestors were slaves, and had been made slaves perhaps by one's own ancestors, to *feel* what I am talking about, which is not at all a personal shame but a racial albatross.

[7] Davey, *op. cit.*, pp. 65, 71.

So this poem poses, if you like, a problem in communication, and first of all to the one person to whom alone it's ostensibly written. I'm grateful, and lucky perhaps, that he liked it and that a much more impartial critic, the black poet-editor of the leading West Indian magazine, *Bim,* approved enough to give it its first publication; within a few months it also appeared in a British journal and before long in both Canadian and American ones.

A poet has to balance such meagre achievements against the failures. A Canadian with the exalted title of High Commissioner to the West Indies saw the poem in the West Indian magazine, and wrote me an emotional and bitter letter. I had, it seems, set back the cause of peace between whites and blacks in the Caribbean a whole generation by publicly crawling before a black man. This High Commissioner was himself a writer of sorts as well as, naturally, a white man, and before he had become High he had been friendly to me and even admiring. But my poetry this time failed to communicate; it gave him no sense of historic guilt for our race, or any share in that sudden moment of curious exaltation and humility I had felt at four o'clock on a Jamaican morning, dancing with my beautiful black friends. Instead, "For George Lamming" ended communications between us for good.

Nevertheless, over the years I've become satisfied with the reception given the piece. It's been made into an Italian poem by a fine writer,[8] been translated into French and Spanish, and been reprinted in a great number of anthologies which circulate it in all parts of the English-speaking world. But what I treasure are the moments when an individual human being — black, white, brown, or rainbow-coloured — comes up to me wherever I may have read the poem and tells me that it's meant something living and true to him or her, as it has to me.

So, in the end, my talk about poetry returns to the reading of it, to the word as a spoken art and an act of brotherhood. It's true I go on writing poems, sending them out to editors, bringing out new books, using the visual couriers of speech. Indeed, in the last fifteen years I've become increasingly interested in

[8] Giose Rimanelli, *Carmina Blabla* (Padua: Rebellato, 1967).

the appearance of my poems on the page, in illustrative drawing, in the patterning of single words photographed and pre-
sented as a colour slide, or in the fusion of type and drawing
— the world of what is loosely called "concrete" poetry. The
"shapome" *first aid* is an example of the sort of poetry that
interests me now:

```
                          •
                          •
                          •

        d               t               d
        e                               e
        i               h               e
        d                               n
    o   b               e           e   s
        m                               o
        e           i   b   s           t
        s               t   e           i
        i                               u
        d       f   o       m   o   s   q
                    T       E
                    O       B

        a   r   c   s       f   i   n   g
        t           •   •           e
        c                           r
        h               •           s
        e                           o
        d                           f
    t y b                           p   o   e   t
    h                                           r
    e                                           y
```

first aid
1972

Yet all my word-building is founded, as in the beginning, on air, on the rhythms and sounds of my words, heard in the inner ear and spoken as well as I'm able to those who will listen.

I go wandering, looking for listeners on campuses in South America, in British pubs and workmen's halls, in Canadian and American schools and colleges and be-ins. As I write this last page I'm rounding up old poems and new, slides and scribbles, to start three months of wandering through Commonwealth countries in Asia and Africa, sounding the "poor words . . . I might have thrown . . . away, / And been content to live." None of us wants merely to live but to affirm life. We all need the therapy of fancy and play, honest emotion, pity, laughter, joy. Especially the joy that comes when the words move someone else from mere living to being Alive, Alive-O!

Available Texts of Poems Discussed in Chapter 3

1. VANCOUVER LIGHTS   The text of this poem is available in my Selected Poems (Toronto: McClelland and Stewart, 1966), and in Poetry of Mid-Century, ed. Milton Wilson (Toronto: McClelland and Stewart, 1964); also, with teaching notes, in Twentieth Century Poetry and Poetics, ed. Gary Geddes (Toronto: Oxford University Press, 1969).

2. MAPPEMOUNDE   This poem failed to gain acceptance from any Canadian magazine when I sent it out; it was first published in an Oklahoma quarterly and first read aloud at a Utah writers' conference. Once it had appeared in my Strait of Anian, 1948, it caught on, and has been anthologized about a dozen times. It is presently available in my Selected Poems; Mandel; Wilson; A. J. M. Smith's Oxford Book of Canadian Verse (Toronto: Oxford University Press, 1965); revised text in Ralph Gustafson's Penguin Book of Canadian Verse (London: Penguin Books, 1967).

3. FROM THE HAZEL BOUGH   Available in the following texts: How Do I Love Thee, ed. J. R. Colombo (Edmonton: M. G. Hurtig, 1970); Mandel, Fifteen Canadian Poets, eds. Gary Geddes and Phyllis Bruce (Toronto: Oxford University Press, 1971); and my Selected Poems and Poems of Earle Birney (Toronto: McClelland and Stewart, 1969).

4. CANADA: CASE HISTORY   Available with notes in the following Toronto-published texts: Voices of Literature, ed. Marshall McLuhan (Holt, Rinehart and Winston of Canada Ltd., 1964); Fifteen Winds, ed. Al Purdy (Toronto: Ryerson, 1967); The Blasted Pine, ed. F. R. Scott (Toronto: Macmillan, 1957); Profile of a Nation, ed. Alan Dawe (Toronto: Macmillan, 1969); What Do You Think?, ed. C. M. Worsnop (Toronto: Copp Clark, 1969); Quest, ed. Wm. Eckersley, (Toronto: Dent, 1970); Generation Now, eds. R. Woolatt and R. Souster (Toronto: Longman of Canada Ltd., 1970).

5. ELLESMERELAND I   This poem is in print in Mandel's Five Modern Canadian Poets, p. 13; my Selected Poems, p. 22; the Poems of Earle Birney, p. 60.

6. EL GRECO: ESPOLIO   The date of the composition of this poem was 1960, as indicated in my Selected Poems, not 1969, as given in Mandel. The text is available in both these books, also in my Poems of Earle Birney and in several current anthologies.

7. A WALK IN KYOTO   Published first in the United States and England. To be found in my Selected Poems and Poems of Earle Birney; Mandel; Wilson; the two Geddes anthologies.

8. SIX-SIDED SQUARE: ACTOPAN   After five years of rejections this poem was first launched in an American journal. It is currently in my Selected Poems; Mandel; and Wilson.

9. SINALOA   Available in my Selected Poems and, with helpful comments, in Mandel; also in 1967 revision of F. R. Scott's The Blasted Pine,

and A. J. M. Smith's *Modern Canadian Verse* (Toronto: Oxford University Press, 1967).

10. FOR GEORGE LAMMING This poem is available in my *Near False Creek Mouth* (Toronto: McClelland and Stewart, 1964) as well as in my *Selected Poems* and *Poems of Earle Birney*; Mandel; Wilson; Geddes. There has been some spatial rearrangement of lines to signal more clearly the rhythm and breath pauses since the 1964 version, but no changes in wording. The poem's first publication was in a Barbadian journal, *Bim*, No. 10 (1964), p. 138.

Appendix A: Extracts From Letters About "David"

1. Teacher, Nova Scotia: "I'm in a quandary. My Grade XI boys are very alert and in their discussion of . . . 'David' they . . . have been involved in lively arguments on some matters pertaining to it.

a. Did Bobby push David over the ledge?

b. What does the 'IT,' which he fears he will see, mean? Why does he fear it?

Personally, I cannot feel that Bob would be such an admirable character if he DID push his friend over, even though the latter did beg for release from anguish. Again why should Bob hurry so for help unless he hoped David would live until help came?" (May, 1957)

Answer: ". . . You are the first teacher I have heard from who has not understood that Bobby did indeed push David over. However, it's no good my telling you; you must read the poem more carefully, and get the evidence from *it* . . ."

2. Quebec Separate high school student: "Dear Mr. Birney, I have been instructed by my literature teacher to write a biography of your life. Because there is a shortage of material for this in our library, I have written to you. What kind of stories do you enjoy writing best? Why do most pupils not like literature? Do you realize that most pupils write what they call garbage on Lit. exams, get marks while those who write what they think get lower marks. Did you ever have the problem of deciding whether to write and say what the teacher wants or what you thought was right? Could you supply some information about influences? Do you think about style, detail, ect. [*sic*] as you write? Yours sincerely." (April 24, 1966)

Answer: "Yes."

3. Class in London, Ont., high school: "We have been assigned to give a seminar on you and your poem 'David.' We are looking forward to reading it but first our English teacher . . . suggested we try and write to the poet himself . . . May we have a picture of you . . . We are doing one seminar pos-

sibly about January 18 or 19 and, if at all possible, would you answer this before then."

Answer: "Your letter received Jan. 18. Let me know if you found time to read the poem. My picture is on the jacket of my *Selected Poems,* on sale in your city's bookstores." (1968)

4. Poet and professor of geography: "The slow passage of time from Summer to Autumn as the lure of the Finger becomes irresistible adds to the solemnity of the drama — it is given a big stage; time passes through it with indifferent grandeur . . . In such a world, unmoved and unmovable, the slip is unforgivable and without mortal remedy . . . the problem of the inexpressible significance of life and the insignificance of men; of being valueless except in well-being; of humanity measuring up to the yardstick of nature." (March, 1942)

5. Manitoba high school student: "The first two stanzas and the title suggested to me the story of David in Biblical times . . . In one incident it took a single stone, in the other a mountain . . . to strengthen the bond of friendship between two boys (David and King Saul; David and Bob)." (1960)

Appendix B: Notes on Notes on "David"

(with special reference to *Longer Poems* / Notes / Birney: "David." Toronto: Coles Pub. Co., 1964)

arête: not just a "ridge" but "an acute and rugged crest of a mountain range" *(Webster's Collegiate)*; French for fishbone

bergschrund: not a "gulf of the gap" (Coles), whatever that means, nor simply a "deep crevice" but the particular chasm, generally widest and deepest of all crevasses, created where the top of the glacier pulls or melts away from the rock of the mountain; what Bob calls a "grave-cold maw"; German for mountain-cleavage

bighorns: not moose, elk, deer or goat, but Rocky Mountain (wild) sheep

cairn: heap of stones on a peak made by climbers to shelter a written record of successful climbs

Cambrian waves: not "curves in the rock" but a reference to the earliest inhabited seas, whose clay shores, pressed to slate, preserved imprints of primitive organisms, the first fossils, now items of our Information Culture; actually I should have said Devonian or Jurassic for the Banff area, but I preferred the sound of "Cambrian."

chimney: some understanding of this mountaineering term is necessary; a vertical rock-cleft wide enough to allow insertion of all or part of the body and facilitate climbing

cirque: circular or semi-circular valley gouged out of a mountain's flank by earlier glacial action

col: the pass or low-point of a ridge between two peaks

coltish: not "coldish" (Coles) but youthful

edgenail: specially tempered steel nails studding soles and edges of climbers' boots

fist (of Mount Finger): not "fish in a frozen ocean of rock" (Coles) or "first" (typographical error in first printing of *David and Other Poems*) but *fist*

flagged: not "shadowed in places" (Coles) but *plumed* (by the small condensation clouds that often stream to leeward from high mountain tops)

gentian: an alpine flower; see dictionary

gyrating: here, the peculiar spiralling motion of a bird with a broken wing *ice axe*: a short-handled tempered-steel instrument with a notched pick point and a blade head; used sometimes on rock but mainly to cut steps on glaciers

larches: not "pines" (Coles) but larches, sometimes called tamaracks; unlike pines they are deciduous, shedding their needles; consequently in high altitudes they look skeletal, "spectral," by September

loose: to loose a hold or a rope means to let it go, not to lose it (Coles); the confusion of these two very different words is one of the many results of sloppy attitudes to the teaching of spelling in schools

marten, moraine, névé, scarp, snout, trilobites: these words deserve to be properly understood; any school dictionary should be adequate, if a textbook isn't

prairie: not "the fields stretching below" (Coles) but the Alberta prairie, commencing seventy miles to the east and visible from the highest peaks around Banff

saxifrage: a note saying this is a "flower" is both superfluous and inadequate; it is a plant that wedges itself into cracks on high rockfaces, a lovely "innocent" whose very act of living is also an act of destruction; a Germanic word meaning "rock-breaker"

serac: a pillar or mound of ice weathered out on the surface of a glacier

snowbridge: when water, melted in the daytime, courses over the top of a glacier and down into crevasses, it often hollows out bridges of snow or ice; some are strong enough to permit the passage of climbers; without such a bridge it is particularly difficult to cross a *bergschrund*

survey: this could scarcely be a job in "open land . . . dividing it into sections with roads at intervals" (Coles) — a strictly Eastern concept; the story is taking place in high mountain wilderness; the survey could be of forest or water and power resources, or of the feasibility of opening up a tourist road; in 1921 I worked on a party which did all these things, in Waterton Park

traverse: (never footnoted); a climbers' term for horizontal routes across peaks or ranges

Appendix C: Bibliographical Information

1. BOOKS IN PRINT

The Creative Writer. Toronto: Canadian Broadcasting Corporation, 1966. (Revised radio talks on writing novels, poems, etc.)
Near False Creek Mouth. Toronto: McClelland and Stewart, 1964. (Poems)
The Poems of Earle Birney. Toronto: McClelland and Stewart, 1969.
Rag&bone Shop. Toronto: McClelland and Stewart, 1971. (Poems)
Selected Poems. Toronto: McClelland and Stewart, 1966.
Turvey. Toronto: McClelland and Stewart, 1949. (Novel)

2. AVAILABLE TAPES & RECORDINGS

Canadian Poets on Tape: "Earle Birney," ½ hr. Toronto: Ontario Institute for Studies in Education, 1969. (Includes "From the Hazel Bough," "For George Lamming." Reading and commentary by author.)
David. Photofolios, Creston, B.C., 1962; 45 RPM, ¼ hr. Reading by author. Obtainable from author, 2030 Barclay St., Vancouver 5, B.C.
David, read by René Auberjonois. LP 33⅓. Order M336, Disc 2, side 2. In sleeve of *Some Haystacks Don't Even Have Any Needle,* an anthology of contemporary poetry, ed. Stephen Dunning. New York: Lothrop, Lee & Shepard Co., 1969.
New Canadian Poets' Series in Cassettes. "Earle Birney," 1 hr. Toronto: High Barnet Co., 1970. (Includes "El Greco: Espolio," "From the Hazel Bough," "Sinaloa," "Vancouver Lights.") Author's reading and commentary.

3. SELECTED CRITICISM

New, Wm. H. "Maker of Order, Prisoner of Dreams: The Poetry of Earle Birney," *Articulating West.* Toronto: New Press, 1972.

110

Robillard, Richard. *Earle Birney*. New Canadian Library, 9. Toronto: McClelland and Stewart, Ltd., 1971.

West, Paul. "Earle Birney and the Compound Ghost," *Canadian Literature* 13 (Summer 1962), 5-14.

Wilson, Milton. "Poet without a Muse," *Canadian Literature* 30 (Autumn 1966), 14-20.

4. BIBLIOGRAPHY

Noel-Bentley, Peter C. "Earle Birney: A Bibliography in Progress, 1923-1969," *West Coast Review* 2 (Oct. 1970), 45-53.

Appendix D: Biographical Note

Earle Birney was born in Calgary, Alta. in 1904. He holds the following degrees: B.A. (U.B.C.); M.A., Ph.D. (Toronto); LL.D. (Alta.); F.R.S.C. He has taught English at the Universities of California (Berkeley and Irvine), Utah, Oregon, Toronto and British Columbia. He was the first to initiate Writers' Workshops at the University of Toronto, 1941, and founded the first independent Department of Creative Writing at the University of British Columbia, 1963. From 1965-1967, he was the University of Toronto's first writer-in-residence.

Earle Birney's poetry readings have taken him across Canada, through the United States, Latin America, Great Britain, France, Australia, New Zealand, Asia and Africa.

His awards include a Canada Council Medal, the Lorne Pierce Medal, two Governor General's awards for poetry, the Stephen Leacock Award and the Borestone Mt. Poetry First.

For further details consult either *Contemporary Poets of the English Language* (London and Chicago: St. James Press, 1970), or the *Canadian Who's Who*.